DATE DUE

NOV

To Serve as Jesus Did

To Serve as Jesus Did

A Ministerial Model for Worship Teams and Leaders

martyHAUGEN

 GIA Publications, Inc.
Chicago

Book layout and design: Nikki Wilkens

G-6705
GIA Publications, Inc.
7404 S. Mason Ave.
Chicago, IL 60638
© 2005 by GIA Publications, Inc.
All rights reserved.
ISBN: 1-57999-537-3

Dedication

To Gwen Haugen,
loving mother, faithful servant

Contents

Foreword

Community worship, especially the Sunday eucharistic gathering, is central to Christian faith formation and growth. Those who prepare and lead worship have a great responsibility and a challenging call. Worship leadership today is complicated by the increasing focus in many churches on elements that are not at the heart of the liturgy. When musical styles, instruments, and electronic media become more important than the Word proclaimed and the Meal shared, worship teams and leaders must ask themselves if they are planning and leading faithfully.

This book evolved over twelve years of full-time music ministry, twenty subsequent years of workshops and conferences with those who lead others in worship, and through conversations with colleagues, mentors, and students. It tries to address a number of concerns raised by individuals seeking to be faithful and effective Christian servants to their communities:

- How can worship be faithful to the Word and rite yet deeply engaged in the life of the world?

- How does one develop and nurture individual musical and speaking skills while evoking and supporting the assembly's song and prayer?

- Is there a conflict between performance and ministry?

- How can a minister know whether he or she is preparing and leading worship in a manner that is both faithful and relevant to God's work in the world?

The model of ministry proposed in this book is based upon the life and teaching of Jesus as presented through the Gospels. The various chapters also reflect the four-fold movement and shape of the Sunday eucharistic celebration—Gathering, Word, Meal, and Sending. It is my belief that this ancient pattern can also give an ever-evolving shape to how we develop and practice our ministry.

I am indebted to many teachers, colleagues and friends who have inspired, challenged, and supported me over the years. I want to thank Alec Harris and GIA Publications for continuing to support my work. Thanks also to my colleague Pastor Susan Briehl for offering suggestions on an early version of the book. I am grateful to editors Vicki Tufano and Elizabeth Dallman Bentley. Finally, my wife and companion, Linda, who did a close reading of the book, continues to be a rock of support and a song of joy.

– Marty Haugen

Worship, Ministry, and Community Life

1

"Teach me thy ways, O Lord" is, like all prayers, a rash one.[1]
— Annie Dillard

A Christian life is forged, defined, and nurtured in relationships. First of all is the relationship with God in Christ through the Spirit, then the relationship with all people and all creation, which bears the sacred presence of God. These relationships are lived out moment by moment by moment. Just as the lover chooses many times within each day to speak and act and live in a way that respects, supports, and cherishes the beloved, so it is for the Christian in relationship to God and all creation.

Living out these relationships is a lifelong passage—sometimes joyous, sometimes wrenching—from repentance to forgiveness, from brokenness to wholeness, from death to new life in Christ. And although it is often a difficult and lonely journey, it is never a journey taken alone. The Christian community pledges to make this pilgrimage with all who would claim the name and the Gospel of Jesus. Through grace, prayer, study, service, and reflection within the support of a loving community, the Christian is called and led to be more and more the image of God's own child in thought, word, and action.

In baptism, we are welcomed into the Body of Christ, the Church, and called to serve one another and, indeed, all people. Our common call to serve, nurture, honor, and support others in the name of Jesus is how *ministry* will be defined throughout this book. Although a *minister* is often defined as one who has been formally trained and, perhaps, ordained to serve a community, it is clear that Jesus intended all of his followers to minister to each other.

THE SUNDAY GATHERING

Each Sunday for nearly 2,000 years, Christian communities have gathered to recall and celebrate their common baptismal covenant, to hear and remember their common stories, to share the pilgrims' sacred meal together, and then to be sent into the world to proclaim and live the Gospel in their own lives. For most of us, it is the Sunday gathering that most powerfully shapes how we understand God, our relationship to God, and our sacred relationship to one another. We who plan and lead worship cannot be faithful in our service to our communities unless our own formation has given us a deep understanding and love of the Word and the tradition of Christian prayer.

Ministry, like medicine or law, is a practice. And, like medicine or law, the ministry of leading a community's common prayer requires study in various disciplines (such as theology, scripture, music, and communication) and training in specific skills (preaching, proclaiming, singing, and playing, to name a few). Without this study and training, we cannot hope to lead our communities confidently or to inspire them in their own ministries.

The practice of ministry is, however, also about the continuing growth and development of the minister. We cannot speak about ministry as if it represented the end of all training. Effective ministers of the Gospel continually grow in their own faith through their openness to new insights, continuing study, and the constant experience of praying with others.

It is easy to define ministry by what we do: a presider leads prayer and preaches; the music minister sings or plays; a lector reads; a catechist teaches; and so forth. Such a definition simplifies our responsibilities. We choose our task, we attend rehearsals, and then we "minister." From this perspective, musical talent, public speaking skills, or teacher training is all that is required.

In reality, the path of the minister is much more. It is a lifelong, life-changing response to God's call to discipleship. It is not about meeting our needs; it is about responding to God's call to share the Gospel—the good news—in all its fullness. Understanding and accepting the difference between ministry as an activity and ministry as a way of being will profoundly change our formation as liturgical ministers and our own faith journey.

The liturgy is the summit toward which the activity of the Church is directed;
it is also the fount from which all her power flows.

– The Constitution on the Sacred Liturgy
(*Sacrosanctum Concilium*), no. 10

THE PRACTICE OF MINISTRY

We choose to serve within our parish communities for a wide variety of reasons. We may join parish music groups or become catechists because we are looking for a chance to meet new people or to share our faith. We may become lectors or cantors because we are looking for an opportunity to speak or sing publicly to a more-or-less attentive audience. Some of us join church music groups because singing is an important part of our prayer lives and we experience the congregation as an inhospitable place to sing. Professional musicians find that parish music positions provide a rare opportunity in today's world: a steady music job that actually pays (if only marginally well). And a few of us become liturgical ministers because we genuinely have experienced a call to give more of ourselves to the community with which we pray. In reality, the reasons we join a particular ministry are not as important as the reasons we stay and how we practice our ministry.

The life and work of every liturgical minister find their deepest meaning within the weekly rhythm of the community's prayer—when God's Word of Life is proclaimed, claimed, and lived out in our midst, when we together celebrate the Feast of Life, meeting at table with Jesus. Indeed, praying the liturgy is itself a central part of the minister's formation. As we pray, so we live; as we live, so we pray.

JESUS AS A MODEL FOR MINISTERS

In searching for an appropriate model for the liturgical minister, we cannot do better than to consider the life and ministry of Jesus. As the minister *par excellence*, Jesus was present and attentive to the needs of those around him while always pointing past himself to his God. His stories and teachings directed his listeners to set their hearts and minds on God (Matthew 5:16; 6:9–10; 12:50). In his miracles and his healings, Jesus deflected attention from himself, giving thanks to God (Matthew 9:8; John 7:16; 9:3–4; 11:41–42) or praising the faith of those who sought him (Matthew 15:28; Mark 5:34).

We can recognize a number of distinctive characteristics in Jesus' life and work. I have identified seven characteristics of Jesus' ministry that can provide a model of how our own ministry might be both faithful to a living tradition and relevant within a rapidly changing world. Of course, these characteristics of Jesus' ministry are not exhaustive. They are also not independent of each other; rather, each supports and evokes the others. They are characteristics that all Christians, regardless of their particular ministries, are called to embody.

Jesus was always present to those around him, and his words and actions were directed by his awareness of God's presence.

Jesus gave his complete attention to each person he encountered (Mark 3:34; 10:21). Because he saw God's presence in every person and in every situation, his ministry was not limited by traditional religious conventions or practices. He was always open to ways in which God might call him to deeper understanding and service (Matthew 8:10; Mark 14:36), and he stressed the critical importance of being present to God's wisdom (Matthew 13:13–17) wherever it is to be found.

Jesus' ministry began with a call to conversion and was marked by continuing conversion.

The first words Jesus speaks in Mark's Gospel (Mark 1:15) are a call to conversion. They come *before* the call to follow him (Mark 1:17). Jesus himself knew the experience and the importance of conversion (Mark 7:24–30). It is clear that the process of continuing conversion, of repeatedly turning toward God and embracing a new life orientation, is essential for those who would follow Jesus.

Jesus' ministry was grounded in and guided by scripture.

Jesus knew the Jewish scriptures well enough to quote them from memory (Matthew 4:4, 7, 10; 21:13; Mark 7:6–10). But scripture for Jesus was more than a series of memorized verses and proverbs. It was a constant companion that guided and shaped his ministry and his own faith life. He quoted scripture not to call attention to himself or his wisdom, but rather to call and challenge his listeners to faithfulness.

Jesus offered each person a genuine and compelling invitation, an invitation that evoked a genuine response.

In the great stories of the Bible—from Abraham and Sarah to Moses, Miriam, and all the prophets—God continually presents individual people with profound and life-changing invitations. In his ministry, Jesus offered the same radical invitation (Matthew 8:19–22; 19:21–22; Luke 9:57–62; John 21:15–19). Whether teaching, healing, or working wonders, Jesus' words and actions represented both an invitation and a challenge. All who accepted his invitation found that they were led into a radically reoriented life.

Jesus was faithful to his religious tradition while always critiquing and challenging it.

The Gospels suggest that Jesus never intended his message or his mission to break from his own Jewish religious tradition (Matthew 5:17–20). Rather, he called his followers to embrace an authentic and profound faithfulness to the religious tradition that formed them. That call is perhaps seen most clearly in the way Jesus shared meals with others. His entire life was a faithful expression of the fundamental Jewish belief (going all the way back to Abraham and Sarah, Genesis 18:1–10) that meals are sacred events—events at which hospitality is central and God is always present, especially in the stranger, the outcast, and the sinner. Indeed, it was Jesus' deep love and faithfulness to the heart of this religious tradition that constantly put him in the position of challenging and critiquing the practices and teachings of religious leaders of his time.

Jesus' ministry focused on and identified with those at the margins of society.

The heart of Jesus' ministry focused on those individuals at the margins of society—the ostracized (Matthew 8:1–4), the hated and shunned (Mark 2:16–17), outsiders and aliens (John 4:1–26), the ailing and vulnerable (John 9:1–7). He understood that the religious life of an individual, a community, or an institution only grew and remained vital through a focus on those at the margins. Indeed, Jesus allowed those very outcasts to be host to him (Luke 7:34; 19:2–10). He understood that God speaks powerfully through those whom "the world" considers of little value. When he addressed the religious leaders of his culture, it was always to call them to a radical engagement with and service to the most powerless and vulnerable.

Jesus' ministry embraced the whole person, body and soul.

Jesus never limited his ministry to an individual's spiritual health. Rather, he healed the sick (Mark 1:40–42), fed the hungry (Matthew 14:14–20), and encouraged and protected the vulnerable and the marginalized (John 8:3–11). His message of salvation and his call to radical conversion could not be separated from his ministry to the very real needs of those he encountered (Mark 1:32). He proclaimed a God who is present in the lament as well as in the hymn of praise, and who is especially receptive to the cries of the oppressed and suffering (Exodus 2:23–25; Sirach 35:15b–26). Jesus also understood the critical importance of the minister's own health, and he sought time for the renewal of his own spirit and body (Matthew 14:13; Mark 1:35; 6:31; Luke 4:42).

EUCHARIST, THE HEART OF MINISTRY

The community's central act of prayer cannot be separated from any of the other ministries in which we might participate. Eucharist is at the heart of our teaching ministry, for worship shapes our hearts and minds more deeply than a classroom experience. It also is intertwined with our healing ministries, because each Eucharist offers the healing gift of forgiveness, celebrates our death and new life in Christ, and calls us to minister to others as we would serve Christ. Eucharist is at the center of our ministries of mercy and justice, for at this table God calls us to a radical reorienting of society's values and priorities and a radical elimination of differences of class and ethnicity; at this table, all are equal, and the greatest is the one who serves.

The rest of this book will examine each of these characteristics of ministry in light of the ancient pattern of the Christian Sunday eucharistic celebration gathering, word, meal, and sending.

Gathering: The Many into One
Chapter Two: Presence and Gratitude
Chapter Three: Turning to New Life

The Word: The Community Remembers and Re-members
Chapter Four: Eating the Words
Chapter Five: The Perilous Invitation of the Gospel

The Sacred Meal: Sharing the Feast of Life
Chapter Six: Living Tradition and Living Culture
Chapter Seven: The Marginalized as Hosts and Guests

Sending: Blessed to Be a Blessing
Chapter Eight: Feeding the Whole Body

In an effort to make this book more than a theoretical examination of ministry, each chapter will offer "head work," "heart work" and "handiwork"—practical suggestions for Christian ministers of ways in which their own ministry can be shaped by the example of Jesus' ministry. As Christian disciples and followers of Jesus, our call is to follow Jesus' example—to minister as Jesus did.

---

1. Anne Dillard, *The Anne Dillard Reader* (New York: Harper Perennial, 1994).

GATHERING: THE MANY INTO ONE

2

Presence and Gratitude

Bidden or not bidden, God is present.[1]
                                        – Carl Jung

The weekly Christian gathering, when we gather to share the Word and the Meal of Life, is a primary place of faith formation. All that we do or say—every action, every silence, the environment, our symbols—everything speaks of our understanding of God, how we interact with God and with one another, and how we believe God transforms our lives through the Gospel. Because all of our words and actions carry such weight, we cannot approach this experience casually or carelessly. In our planning and preparations, in our leadership and presentation, we must be wholly present to the community and its prayer, and to God's presence within that prayer.

Good celebrations foster and nourish faith. Poor celebrations may weaken and destroy it.   – *Music in Catholic Worship*, n.6

The ancient yet ever-new rhythm of Christian worship evolves through the constant creative tension between a living tradition handed down from the ancestors and the many cultures that welcome that tradition into their own worlds. The earliest Christians gathered for Eucharist with little formal ritual, probably with singing, a greeting, and prayer. What we would call "gathering rites" emerged gradually, with different elements appearing over centuries from different strains of the Christian tradition. So the *Kyrie* is a gift from the Eastern Churches, while the *Gloria in excelsis* comes to us from the Roman tradition.

Regardless of the elements and forms of the various gathering rites from the various traditions, they evolved for very distinct and specific reasons:

- To create from a diverse (and sometimes divisive) group of individuals a single body, present and ready to hear God's Word and share the sacred Meal of Jesus.
- To help the community recall and renew its common baptismal covenant.
- To connect those gathered (through music, ritual action, and prayer) to the great rhythm of the liturgical seasons and feasts.
- To connect every Christian gathering with the prayer of our ancestors and offer a vision for the future that transcends culture and time.

Gathering rites are intended to create in those who gather an awareness of being deeply present to God and to one another. When we are present to God, open to God's gracious and loving action and to God's healing and nurturing presence in each other, the natural response is a deep sense of gratitude for all of God's blessings. These two attitudes—presence and gratitude—prepare the community to hear God's Word and create a hunger and thirst to share the banquet feast of Jesus together.

PRESENCE

What can we offer each other that is more precious than our presence—our time, our care, and our attention? Whether it is only for a moment—responding to someone in need as we go about our daily tasks—or whether it is a lifetime of attentive love for a partner, parents, or children, being present to others is at the very heart of the Christian way of life. In our presence to others, we discover the sacred nature of relationship and life, and we experience how God comes to us in and through others. Just as we can discover Christ in another, so another can discover Christ through us.

When we listen, serve, and care with our whole hearts and minds we share in a foretaste of God's reign here on earth. In these moments, we experience "Sabbath time," a time not just of rest and renewal, but an opportunity for wonder and joy and deep peace, a moment of eternity opening in the midst of life's distractions and activities.

Think about moments of real presence in our lives—being enchanted by the eyes or laughter of a child; being enfolded in the arms of our beloved; sharing a feast with good friends and family; making music, listening, or counseling; keeping vigil at the bedside of a sick son or daughter, parent, or friend; being absorbed in moments of deep prayer, fear, anger, love, or joy—at these times, the rest of the world drops away, and only this moment, this experience, this person exists. As followers of Jesus, we are called to give this focus and attention to every encounter and each person, with the full awareness that God is present in each human contact and in every human experience. In our service as ministers, we participate in the proclamation and revelation of God's sacred presence through our own holy presence to and with others.

SABBATH TIME

The ancient Greeks used two different words to express their experience of time. *Chronos* refers to the forward movement of time: minutes, hours, days, and years. *Kairos* is time that is always in the present. *Kairetic* time, holy time, Sabbath time, opens like a bud flowering into full bloom. We inhabit *kairetic* time when we are truly present to one another. It might be compared to a holiday family gathering when no one looks at his or her watch, and the passage of *chronos* ceases to matter. We live in the moment, enjoying food, play, conversation, and communion for their own sake.

For many of us, Sunday worship remains *chronos* rather than *kairos*, with the congregation and the leaders of prayer all intently and painfully aware of time passing and the need to complete the service within a specific span of time. In such a situation, *kairetic* time—remaining fully in the present moment—is impossible. Our gathering rituals are an opportunity for us to invite and gently welcome everyone present to move from *chronos* into *kairos*, from the schedules and deadlines that define and control our lives to the luxurious and spacious time of Sabbath.

Perhaps we so rarely experience Sabbath time in worship because it is so lacking in the rest of our lives. The responsibilities of work, relationships, and study, the frenetic pace of our daily world, and the constant and intense bombardment of media can quickly and completely fill every bit of our awareness, leaving little room or energy for simply being present to another or to a moment. When we do have a free moment, often we are too exhausted or distracted to be aware of others and our surroundings.

I suggest that what we need today is a new "mystagogy" in which humankind is guided to a more profound recognition of the presence of God as Holy Mystery emerging from within the warp and woof of our daily lives.[2]
— Richard R. Gaillarde

In her book *Receiving the Day* Dorothy Bass describes the dilemma we face when our sense of sacred, Sabbath time becomes distorted by the rhythms of the work and entertainment and technological culture:

> At the heart of our attitudes and experiences of time are issues of identity and conscience, matters of the spirit...Distortions in the shape of our time foster distortions in the shape of our lives and the quality of all of our relationships. Indeed, these distortions drive us into the arms of a false theology: we come to believe that we, not God, are masters of time.[3]

Sabbath time does not easily coexist with the rhythms of the digital age. Sabbath time is kept by the gentle and unfailing natural rhythms of life and of nature—sunrise and sunset, the changing phases of the moon, and the life-giving cycle of the seasons. These rhythms have marked and ordered human life on this planet for millennia, yet they are largely absent from the lives of many North Americans today. Artificial light permits us to set our own patterns for sleeping and waking; twenty-four-hour television creates the sense that the day never ends; fast food restaurants provide us with instantaneous meals consumed without awareness of their origins and often without the companionship of others; supermarkets, health clubs, and discount stores never close. Air travel allows us to awaken in one time zone and go to sleep eight time zones away, and produce can be shipped so rapidly that it is normal to have our fruits and vegetables out of season. When we lose our sense of these natural rhythms, our lives easily take on a more relentless pace, a pace measured by the quick cuts of a video screen, the non-stop invasion of music into our environment, freeway aggressiveness, and tight schedules.

Countless "labor-saving devices," such as computers, microwave ovens, and cell phones only accelerate the pace of our lives; they blur the distinction between work and play and demean the sacredness of meal and family time. While the speed of the Internet and the convenience of mobile phones have given us communication access undreamed of only a few years ago, they have also exposed us to more stimuli and information than we can possibly retain. These changes increasingly separate us from authentic life experience, separating us from Sabbath time with others. As Richard Gaillarde says in his book *Transforming Our Days*,

> When cell phones, pagers, and notebook computers are purchased in the vain hope that they can free us from the confines of the office, it is far more likely the case that they have simply *extended* office boundaries to include car and home, thereby robbing us of any remaining private space for family and recreation...We...need a heightened attentiveness to the overarching influence of technology and consumerism on the contours and rhythms of our daily existence...the discernment demanded of us is a "lifestyle" discernment, not a discernment about the goodness or badness of a particular device.[4]

Gaillarde maintains that even though technology has increasingly fragmented and distorted our life experiences, we cannot simply blame technology or our work schedules for the distracted nature and chaos of our lives. Rather than simply rejecting technology or running away from responsibility, we need to re-order the way we look at time. As Dorothy Bass puts it, "We need to learn a richer language than the language of management. We need to develop life patterns that get us through our days not only with greater efficiency but also with greater authenticity as human beings created in God's image."[5]

The frenetic and often chaotic lives that we lead through the rest of the week make the creation of Sabbath time within our worship both critically important and more difficult. Every aspect of our gathering—from the moment people enter the church through the opening prayer that marks the transition into the Liturgy of the Word—can help move us from *chronos* to *kairos*. In the space of about five minutes (*chronos* time) our tasks are to:

- Gather the many into one,
- Prepare the community to pray with understanding and enthusiasm,
- Mark our common baptismal covenant,
- Draw the community into the season or feast we are about to celebrate, *and*
- Create a sense of sacred presence.

Beyond the distractions and frenetic rhythms of the larger world, our very work as ministers can also keep us from being present to the real needs of those within and around our community. When we get caught up in our activities, schedules, rehearsals, performances, or presentation style, we quickly lose the ability to be truly present to others within our worship, or present to the One who promises to come to us in Word and Meal and in those with whom we pray. If this happens, we not only miss the gift that others may bring to us, but miss the opportunity to experience God's presence in our encounters with others, both inside and outside worship.

Without a sense of presence to others, our ministry quickly loses it meaning and degenerates into self-gratification and self-interest. Recovering the critical place of Sabbath time in our own lives will help us order our responsibilities in a way that honors God's sacred presence in others and our experiences with them.

THE MINISTER'S CALL TO SACRED PRESENCE

In our baptism we share in Christ's death and rising. As we are marked with the sign of the cross, we are each called into a life of service to others in the name and the spirit of Jesus. In our service, we seek to recognize, proclaim, and celebrate the presence of Christ always and everywhere. This lifelong vocation begins with our attentiveness to others. Before we can serve others, we need to know them, their needs, and their gifts.

[Jesus said to his disciples]..."Remember, I am with you always, to the end of the age."

– Matthew 28:20b

The Risen Christ has promised to be present to and with us in a limitless number of ways—through every experience, through a myriad of cultural and religious expressions. The many meanings of the phrase "real presence" invite and challenge us to consider the ways that God's presence is experienced (or missed) inside and outside our worship celebrations. The words also remind us that just as Christ is present to us we are also called to be present to God's Spirit at work in our lives and in the lives of others.

It is not unusual for Christians to believe that achieving a sense of the sacred requires us to leave the "ordinary" world behind. Many of us make a sharp division between "sacred" and "secular" experience. We may come to believe that the stuff of the world in its ordinariness is something other than holy. But Jesus chose simple and ordinary things to reveal God's holy presence and Spirit at work—mud (John 9:6–7), soil (Matthew 13:3–9), water (John 2:6–11), seeds (Mark 4:30–32), grain (Mark 4:1–9), and bread (Matthew 15:32–37).

Although we often divide our life experiences into "sacred" and "secular" categories, God has declared all of creation "good" or "holy" (Genesis 1:31). A "secular" understanding of creation is a human distortion of nature's way—of God's way. Indeed, it is just this understanding—of a "secular" or less-than-sacred universe—that has given many humans a rationale to exploit and ravage much of our environment. People who would be scandalized by wanton vandalism and destruction in a "sacred" church sanctuary accept the irresponsible waste and exploitation of the "secular" earth as progress, development, and a God-given right. We can learn much from native peoples around the world whose belief systems proclaim their sacred and mutually dependent relationship to the entire universe. Indeed, they might lead us to recover and reclaim a biblical understanding of the sacredness of creation and our role as stewards of it.

When we recognize all of creation as holy, we can no longer justify a careless or exploitive relationship to the world and its creatures. Such a worldview calls us to be careful stewards of both space and time. The world is sacred, and our life here—the time we spend here—is also sacred.

When we have a sense of all creation as sacred space, worship ceases to be an island of sacredness in a secular world. We can accept mistakes and interruptions within prayer, seeing them not as incidents that destroy the sense of the sacred, but as one more expression of God's presence. The noise of an infant in worship becomes a sign of God's sacred life, coughing simply represents the frailty to the body, and sirens passing by become an awareness of how our prayers must encompass the larger world.

Just as we often do not recognize the sacredness of the world around us, we can easily forget or deny that God's Spirit is present in people we find objectionable or socially less desirable. While Jesus recognized God's sacred presence in everyone, he most often focused his attention on those people whom the religious leaders of his society had excluded or marginalized—a woman divorced four times (John 4:1–39), a man afflicted with an incurable, contagious, and socially stigmatizing disease (Matthew 8:1–4), a man who was mentally unstable and behaved inappropriately in public (Mark 5:1–13), an adulteress (John 8:1–11), prostitutes (Matthew 21:31), and those whom we name as enemies. While Jesus did not excuse sinful behavior, he recognized God's sacred presence in each individual and gave his undivided, compassionate attention to them and to their needs. Those of us in leadership positions within liturgy can easily get caught up in the "details," forgetting that ministry begins with the act of being deeply present to all those inside and outside our communities. Indeed, it is only through giving our real presence to others that we discover and renew our vocation and vision.

This means that all of our worship, beginning with our gathering rites, must clearly name and affirm that when we seek to be present to God our focus is not only inward but also outward to all those uncomfortable places and people in which and in whom we continually encounter the presence of the Risen Christ. Being present to God and also being aware of God's presence in others are not really two separate activities. Jesus taught that in our attention to others and to their needs we are truly being present to God.

*The king will say to those at his right hand, "Come, you that are blessed . . .
for I was hungry and you gave me food, I was thirsty and you gave me
something to drink, I was a stranger and you welcomed me, I was naked
and you gave me clothing, I was sick and you took care of me, I was in
prison and you visited me." Then the righteous will answer him, "Lord,
when was it that we saw you hungry and gave you food, or thirsty and
gave you something to drink? And when was it that we saw you a stranger
and welcomed you, or naked and gave you clothing? And when was it that
we saw you sick or in prison and visited you?" And the king will answer
them, "Truly I tell you, just as you did it to one of the least of these who
are members of my family, you did it to me."*

– Matthew 25:34–40

In difficult and stressful times when we are busy with many things, it is
easy to lose a sense of God's presence. But God is never absent from us;
rather, we become so preoccupied with other things that we lose our awareness
of God's constant presence. To be an effective minister, we must first be
grounded in the present moment, so that we can be open to God's quiet
but constant presence, in others and in our experiences with others.

There are active and receptive dimensions to being present. These
two dimensions could be compared to intellectual and emotional activities.
The active, intellectual side of presence means that we give our full attention
to others, looking and listening consciously and deliberately, seeking to
hear and understand who they are and what they are communicating.
This means speaking less and listening more; it means reserving our opinions
and comments until we truly hear the other person—not merely their
words, but their feelings and perspectives. We engage our mind for
understanding rather than for putting forth our own ideas.

But there is also a receptive dimension to presence. Not only do we
give our presence to others, but we also open ourselves to receive God's
sacred presence through them. Emotionally, this requires a heart that is
grateful, free of envy or self-interest. By remembering the gifts that have
been showered upon us, we can allow ourselves gratefully to receive the
Spirit's presence—through others' joys and sorrows and challenges.

I pray that the God of our Lord Jesus Christ, the Father of glory, may give you a spirit of wisdom and revelation as you come to know him, so that, with the eyes of your heart enlightened, you may know what is the hope to which he has called you, what are the riches of his glorious inheritance among the saints, and what is the immeasurable greatness of his power for us who believe, according to the working of his great power.

– Ephesians 1:17–19

To open the "eyes of our hearts" is to be receptive to how God's Spirit is constantly at work in our lives, especially in our encounters with others. It is a receptiveness that must be continuously nurtured through prayer and practice. Our responsibilities, deadlines, frustrations, and distractions will not cease; they will continue to draw the eyes of our hearts away from this moment and this experience of presence. To fashion Sabbath time in the midst of digital time, we must establish a rhythm of Sabbath—morning or evening prayer, meals that are eaten with a sense of reverence and delight, work and play given their own space and attention.

Cherishing and nurturing our own prayer life can improve our ability to be present to others. Broadening our understanding of sacred time, sacred place, and sacred encounter, we can come to know more deeply the holiness of being present to others and their needs.

The busy lives that all of us lead can make achieving and maintaining a sense of presence and awareness difficult. Here is a strategy based on two distinct but complementary elements of presence—attention and gratitude.

HEAD WORK: ATTENTION

One day a man said to Zen Master Ikkyu: "Master, will you please write for me a maxim of the highest wisdom?" Ikkyu immediately took his brush and wrote the word "Attention." "Is that all?" asked the man. "Will you not add something more?" Ikkyu then wrote twice running: "Attention. Attention." "Well," remarked the man rather irritably, "I really don't see much depth or subtlety in what you have just written." Then Ikkyu wrote the same word three times running: "Attention. Attention. Attention." Half-angered, the man demanded: "What does that word 'Attention' mean anyway?" And Ikkyu answered gently: "Attention means attention."[6]

– From the Zenso Mondo Dialogues of the Zen Masters

Peter looked intently at [the lame man], as did John, and said, "Look at us." And he fixed his attention on them, expecting to receive something from them. But Peter said, "I have no silver or gold, but what I have I give you; in the name of Jesus Christ of Nazareth, stand up and walk."

– Acts 3:4–6

Here are some simple "head work" exercises intended to help bring the mind back to the true attentiveness that every minister needs in order to be present to others. Every person's life is unique; undertake these exercises in a way that respects your own situation. Do not let the exercises be one more task in your life; rather, explore how you can practice these suggestions in a way that is natural and supportive of your life as it is.

Simplify and prepare.

We liturgical ministers constantly try to do more and bigger things. In doing so, we can easily lose sight of what is important. For example, we might have big, beautiful musical events during Advent and at Christmas and wonder afterwards why we were not able to pray. In that case, perhaps we need to simplify the musical elements of our community's prayer to the point that we can be so thoroughly prepared that we are able to move past ourselves and our performance to focus on the community and their prayer. Preparing more thoroughly for rehearsals and introducing less new music will allow us to be more attentive to the music, to the other members of our music ministry, and to our own participation in the community's prayer.

Practice listening skills.

Listen to others. Really listen. Listen and observe with your full attention. Look at people while they speak. Listen to what their expressions and gestures are saying as well as their words. Allow others to speak without interrupting, and try to hear what others are saying rather than planning a response while they are still speaking.

Build in time for prayer each day.

The faith of the Christian is formed over time, like the love of a married couple, through an on-going daily rhythm of attentiveness and faithful sharing. The amount of time that we spend in prayer each day is not as important as the regular rhythm and the quality of presence that we bring to those moments. Reserve some time for prayer each day that is untouchable by other commitments. Spending twenty minutes each day in calm and receptive prayer can become an essential part of a deeper, renewed sense of ministry.

Take your watch off during liturgy.

If we prepare well, don't waste our words or songs, and are truly present to the prayer, it is much easier to release ourselves and invite our communities into *kairos*. Liturgy well prepared and prayed seems to stop time. Those of us who lead worship might consider taking off our watches during liturgy (without using it as an excuse to preach or sing as long as we wish!). The good preparation that's necessary for a *kairetic* experience should also keep us from overindulging ourselves.

HEART WORK: GRATITUDE

For all that has been, "Thanks,"
For all that will be, "Yes."[7]
> – Dag Hammarskjold

Gratitude comes naturally when we approach our experiences with a quiet and attentive mind. When we are open and receptive, we can become aware of the movement of God's grace in our lives, and give thanks for it. This sense of gratitude is essential for our effectiveness as ministers.

A grateful heart has no room for worry and egoism. The one who is grateful for God's gifts rejoices in helping others; such a minister weeps with another's misfortune and delights in another's joys and talents. The minister who gratefully recognizes, remembers, and celebrates God's blessings can easily discern the difference between self-serving performance and gracious ministry to others. Here are some simple suggestions to cultivate gratitude.

Take time to recognize and remember God's gracious activity.

Without a constant remembrance of how God has acted in our lives, we quickly lose an awareness of God's present and continuing action in our lives and in the lives of others. When we forget what God has done for and in us, our ministry becomes empty action rather than life-filled service.

Practice receptive prayer.

Receptive prayer listens and accepts; it does not make requests of God. Receptive prayer is grounded in the belief that God wants what is best for us and for others and that our task is to listen and discern God's active presence in our life experiences. When this belief takes hold of our minds and hearts, gratitude becomes our normal state. Taking time before rehearsals and before liturgy to share with other ministers in prayers of thankfulness and openness to God's spirit can be a valuable help in nurturing a collective sense of gratitude and a deepened sense of ministry.

Find ways to be fed by others in common prayer.

The minister who is always in a leadership role in community prayer can quickly lose an awareness of the importance of being fed by others. Such a minister may even find it difficult to be in a less visible, less responsible role. Finding a time and place to participate in communal prayer as a member of the assembly can be vitally important. Occasionally, when you are not scheduled to minister, pray with another parish community, or find a regularly scheduled morning or evening service during the week where you don't have to serve. Many places have recently begun Taizé-style prayer services; if there's one near you, you may find it a good way to practice receptive prayer.

Note the danger of leading multiple celebrations.

To be completely present for even a short time is extremely difficult; to be totally present through several celebrations is virtually impossible. The minister who attempts this regularly can easily become inattentive and, eventually, uncaring. Many ministers in leadership positions may have little choice in this matter, but an awareness of the problem may give someone in that situation motivation to seek creative ways to limit their responsibility.

HANDIWORK: BEING PRESENT TO LIFE

The greatest revelation is stillness.
— Lao Tsu

These "handiwork" exercises may not seem to be directly related to ministry, but I have found them to be helpful in developing a greater awareness of others and a deeper sense of being present to life.

Widen your circle of the sacred.

Make it your goal (and help to make it the goal of all in your ministry team) to enter into a sense of sacred time and space even before arriving at church. Pick up litter on the way to church, act courteously and hospitably to other drivers on the way, or take an opportunity to do an act of kindness. Use this time to help create an awareness of sacred time and space beyond the boundaries of our narrow vision.[8]

Make room for quiet in your life.

Choose to have silence in your house, car, or office rather than the constant sound of news or music around you. Develop an awareness of the beauty of silence. Try to go a day (or longer) without any electronic media (radio, television, or recordings) so that you might better appreciate the beauty of silence. Try to develop an interior silence as well; see if for a short time each day you can quiet the interior monologue that often runs through your brain. Without some silence, all sound has less value, and we become poorer listeners. You will quickly find that such a quiet time enables you to make better use of the entire day.

Do one thing at a time.

If we do a good job of preparing and simplifying, it becomes possible to focus on doing only one thing at a time. When we eat, we simply eat; we don't watch television or read. When we drive, we simply drive—no eating, no talking on a cell phone. And when we pray, we simply pray, allowing ourselves to be present to every sound and action of the presider, the musicians, the lectors, and the assembly, as well as natural sounds and sights in the worship space. When we are attentive and aware of God's strong presence surrounding us, our ministry becomes an expression of faith-filled gratitude. Only then can we grow in our ministry and our own faith life.

---

1. Psychologist Carl Jung had this carved in Latin over the front door of his Zurich home.
2. Richard Gaillarde, *Transforming Our Days* (New York: Crossroad, 2000), 64.
3. Dorothy Bass, *Receiving the Day* (San Francisco: Jossey-Bass, 2000), 2–3.
4. Gaillarde, 138.
5. Bass, xiii.
6. Quoted in Roshi Phillip Kapleau, *The Three Pillars of Zen* (Garden City, New York: Anchor Books, 1980), 10–11.
7. Dag Hammarskjold, *Markings*, translated by Leif Sjöberg and W. H. Auden (New York: Ballantine Books, 1983).
8. From a suggestion by Fr. Ed Foley, OFM.

Turning to New Life

3

When true simplicity is gained,
to bow and to bend we shan't be ashamed,
to turn, turn will be our delight,
'til by turning, turning we come 'round right.

— Shaker hymn

Honesty can be painful, especially when we're being honest about ourselves. When we honestly confront our words, thoughts, and actions, we realize that we are not yet the children of God we are called to be. Admitting this to God, to one another, and to ourselves is difficult but necessary before God's Spirit can move within us and renew our hearts. This is why liturgical churches provide a place within the gathering rites for individuals and the community as a whole to name and confront their shortcomings, to invoke and receive God's mercy and love, and then to celebrate and praise the One who forgives and strengthens them to live in holiness, joy, delight, and peace.

Whenever we are present to others and to our life experiences, we will inevitably discover God calling us to a deeper and more challenging life of service. Sometimes the call is faint, and often we do not want to hear it. But if we try to be receptive to how God speaks to us, sooner or later we will have to respond to the call.

THE CALL TO CONVERSION

Have you been born again? It is one of those questions that can make us uncomfortable. It usually comes from someone we do not know well, and it can lead to a discussion about what it means to be Christian. Or it can lead to a few embarrassed, mumbled words and a desire to be elsewhere.

Much of the discomfort arises from the different ways that Christians understand the experience of conversion. Many who describe themselves as "born-again Christians" believe that conversion is a single, non-repeatable, personal experience or encounter with Jesus that causes a new and permanent orientation in their lives. It could be described like this:

Encounter with Jesus ➤ Choice to become Christian ➤ New life in Christ

Without denying the validity of this transformation for some, I have come to experience conversion differently. Rather than a one-time, linear experience, I have experienced my faith life as a series of calls to conversion. Each call is both an invitation and a challenge to a more committed following of Jesus. Each invitation requires a response. If I choose to say "yes" to the call, if I turn and take the path that is offered, I am led into a new and deeper life in Christ, one that very often takes me "where I would not choose to go" (John 21:18). If, through grace, I am able to embrace and live this new orientation, I will eventually be faced with another call, and the cycle repeats. At each stage, I have the choice to say yes or no, but if I am truly open and honest with myself, I am unable to deny the invitation. The model looks like this:

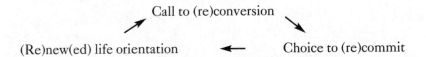

Call to (re)conversion

(Re)new(ed) life orientation ⟵ Choice to (re)commit

Each new call to conversion comes out of a response to the last call. For instance, a parish musician may be challenged by a parishioner or a liturgy or a life experience to examine the words he or she sings more carefully. As a result of studying scripture and critical reflection, the musician feels challenged and called by God to a very different sort of music making in worship. This might involve a different model for choosing music (beginning with scripture rather than musical style), a different model of presenting music (focusing more on the congregation's response than on the performance or image of the musician), and a different model of success (focusing less on personal acclaim or numbers and more on the conversion and renewal of the community). This new experience of worship may elicit another response by a member of the assembly; the musician is challenged anew, and the process repeats.

CONVERSION AND PASSION

True conversion brings new life and passion to the believer. Without this continuous deepening of our response to God's call, we can easily lose our passion and end up going through the motions in our ministry. This can be a problem for liturgical ministers. We who prepare and lead celebrations every weekend (sometimes several times each weekend) often find it difficult to stay passionate and present to the experience. Yet, without real passion for our common prayer and a genuine presence to our community, we will be unable to pray authentically or lead others in authentic prayer.

Walter Brueggemann suggests that the passion that comes from true conversion will often be at odds with our respectable and well-ordered idea of Christian community life. When Christians become comfortable, he says, they also become less comfortable with a passionate God who is likely to call them to care for the marginalized and commit to the transformation of our society:

> Passion as the capacity and readiness to care, to suffer, to die, and to feel is the enemy of imperial reality...Perhaps [we are] so enmeshed in this reality that another way is nearly unthinkable. The dominant history [of our] time consists in briefcases and limousines and press conferences and quotas and new weaponry systems. And that is not a place where much *dancing* happens and where no *groaning* is permitted.[1]

Because worship is a primary place of faith formation, those of us who plan and lead worship are the very ones Brueggemann calls to be prophets, those at the heart of the renewal of the church:

> I suspect that our own self-concept as would-be prophets is most often too serious, realistic, and even grim. The characteristic way of the prophet in Israel is that of poetry and lyric. The prophet engages in futuring fantasy...[I]t is the vocation of the prophet to keep alive the ministry of imagination, to keep on conjuring and proposing alternative futures to the single one the king wants to urge as the only thinkable one.[2]

Replace the word "prophet" with "liturgical minister," and "king" with any symbol of power or the status quo, and we begin to glimpse the challenge to those of us who plan and lead worship. God confronts the committed minister with a never-ending succession of calls (especially through the marginalized within our community and society). Our "yes" to those calls is essential if our ministry and our worship are to remain vital.

Authentic and continuous conversion is neither easy nor comfortable. True conversion opens us to the awareness that God may—and likely will—move us out of our areas of security and familiarity into challenging and life-changing encounters. Jesus' very first words in the Gospel of Mark should be the mantra of every minister: "The time is fulfilled, and the Reign of God is at hand; repent, and believe in the gospel" (Mark 1:15). While repentance here includes the common understanding of turning away from our shortcomings and sins, it goes far beyond that. Repentance repeatedly and radically reorients us to God's vision rather than to our own. This is the real call to discipleship.

Later, at the very heart of Mark's Gospel, Jesus tells his would-be followers just how deep and life-changing the path of the minister is: "[Jesus] called the crowd with his disciples, and said to them, 'If any want to become my followers, let them deny themselves and take up their cross and follow me'" (Mark 8:34).

Jesus speaks to "the crowd" as well as to "his disciples." We can read this distinction to mean that this is a message for everyone who wishes to be a follower of Jesus. The call of the minister (literally, "one who serves") is the proper vocation of every Christian. If we choose to be Christians—if we choose to follow Jesus—we confront this three-fold challenge: to deny ourselves, to take up our cross, and to follow Jesus.

To deny ourselves.

Before Jesus says, "Follow me," he says, "Deny yourself." Our calling is not about what *we* want; it is about what God wants us to be and do. We are often drawn to do a particular ministry—leading prayer through word and music, teaching, counseling, spiritual direction, and healing—because of our particular gifts or talents. But to be a minister is to understand and acknowledge that our specific ministry is only one of a myriad of ways in which we might be called to serve. The call of the Christian is to use one's whole life and all of one's talents to assist in bringing about the fullness of God's Reign. This means letting go of any desire to control or limit how ministry happens and coming to see our treasured gifts and talents simply as tools to bring others to God. We cannot hide behind music stands or organ consoles, microphones or lecterns, "traditional" or "contemporary" music styles, or curricula or scheduled hospital visits, believing that our ministry begins and ends there. Our call is to let God use us, even in ways we do not choose and cannot control (John 21:18).

To take up our cross.

For the community from which the Gospel of Mark arose, the meaning of "to take up your cross"[3] might well have been literal. Many members of that community suffered for their faith, and some died. Today, in North America, most Christians probably do not expect their faith to present them with any great hardships. But to faithfully "take up our cross" will inevitably put us in conflict with much of the prevailing culture's attitudes and beliefs, requiring sacrifices from us that we would rather not make. The road of the faithful minister in our day, as in the time of Jesus and his first followers, is often not an easy or a popular one.

To follow Jesus.

Following Jesus, of course, is the heart of what it means to live as a Christian. But how do we follow Jesus? This question has led to many of the divisions among Christians as people of faith have struggled to respond to the call of Jesus within a particular cultural, historical, or personal perspective. While we may believe that we have a clear understanding of the Christian call and pathway, if we are not open to the Spirit's movement, we can easily come to think that our own desires and agendas are God's.

As ministers, before we learn the chords, before we practice the scales, before we train our speaking voices, we must open ourselves to God's call to service, letting go of our need to perform or be recognized. Over and over again, as we do our ministry, we seek to retain that openness, no matter how challenging and painful. Only then does making music or proclaiming the Word or any service become ministerial and remain spirit-filled. With such openness, our gifts and talents become simply the particular pathways we use to pass on and live the Gospel.

Very truly, I tell you, when you were younger, you used to fasten your own belt and go wherever you wished. But when you grow old, you will stretch out your hands, and someone else will fasten a belt around you and take you where you do not wish to go.

– John 21:18

Perhaps the most important conversion experience for ministers is the hard realization that we are *not* the focus—not our skills, goodness, holiness, or problems. Pastor, presider, music minister, lector, deacon—all of us are called to focus our attention outward in service to others. Such a focus will inevitably allow the Spirit to call us deeper and deeper into the life of Christ, often leading us "where we would rather not go." Although it may be difficult for us to accept, we are not in charge of our own ministries— God is. When we are able to see ourselves honestly, to turn and humbly seek God's mercy and grace, we find that we are freed to love more deeply and compassionately. We are free to follow Jesus more closely.

A woman in the city, who was a sinner, having learned that [Jesus] was eating in the Pharisee's house, brought an alabaster jar of ointment. She stood behind him at his feet, weeping, and began to bathe his feet with her tears and to dry them with her hair. Then she continued kissing his feet and anointing them with the ointment...Turning toward the woman, [Jesus] said to Simon, "Do you see this woman? I entered your house; you gave me no water for my feet, but she has bathed my feet with her tears and dried them with her hair. You gave me no kiss, but from the time I came in she has not stopped kissing my feet. You did not anoint my head with oil, but she has anointed my feet with ointment. Therefore, I tell you, her sins, which were many, have been forgiven; hence she has shown great love. But the one to whom little is forgiven, loves little." Then he said to her, "Your sins are forgiven."

– Luke 7:37–38, 44–48

HEAD WORK: GROWING INTO AN ADULT FAITH

While we may envy those with a simple, child-like faith, adult Christians need a mature faith that can confront the most difficult issues of life—death and separation, injustice and evil, betrayal and abandonment. This type of faith will never take root in us until we accept that God is larger than our own understanding and agendas. Accepting this, we open ourselves to the movement of God's Spirit, especially in ways that we might initially resist. The only certainty for us ministers is that the Gospel of Jesus will call us beyond our comfort zones into a constantly deeper and more expansive understanding of the commitment we make in response to God's call.

HEART WORK: LETTING GO OF BIASES

The faithful servant of Jesus constantly seeks to be open to the Spirit and engaged in God's creation. Too often, we try to limit how the Spirit of God works. We may ignore or reject the possibility that the Spirit could work through other denominations, through other faith traditions, and even through those who reject God and religion out of hand. Many times it is precisely through these people and experiences with them that we can hear God's voice in a new and deeper way. We must develop the eyes to see outside the boxes we try to create for God.

HANDIWORK: EXERCISES TO OPENNESS

Recognizing the Spirit's presence within the challenges of the ministry team.

No minister will remain untouched by the inevitable tensions within parish ministry: between clergy and lay ministers, between directors of ensembles and group members, or among the parish staff. A pastor and a musician may clash over what, how, and when to sing or not sing. One group member may become jealous of the role of another. Some may grow possessive of "their liturgy" or "their celebration." It is important to remember that these situations can offer an opportunity for the movement of God's Spirit, calling us to grow through the hard work of listening to and learning from each other. A required formation evening for all ministers (including clergy) at the beginning of each year can be a time for refocusing and renewing our commitment. Sharing food and conversation and caring among members of a ministerial group and between various ministries can help to open the door for communication. Rotating various music ensembles through the weekend celebrations, although often difficult, helps each ensemble to see its role as one of service to a wider community.

For the pastor and the musician and the liturgist—for all ministers who experience conflict—moving from an adversarial to a collaborative relationship—from a win/lose relationship to a win/win relationship—is absolutely fundamental. It begins with the hard truth that our ministries are not primarily about us; they are about serving the good of the community members so that they, in turn, may serve as they are called.

Recognizing the Spirit's presence in the challenges of the community.

When I worked full-time in parish ministry, I was painfully aware of complaints from members of the community. Too often they came in the form of unsigned letters and anonymous phone messages. It was always tempting to discount the comments of others and take refuge in the belief that my vision was wider and clearer than that of the complainers. However, the Christian minister is called to be open to the possibility that God's Spirit is speaking through every experience, especially the most difficult ones.

Recognizing the Spirit's presence in the wider world.

A community that limits its openness to the members of their own community or those just like them will die. Living and growing communities constantly expand their focus, embracing especially those at the margins of our lives and of our communities. See the HEAD WORK, HEART WORK, and HANDIWORK sections at the end of Chapter Seven for some specific suggestions.

1. Walter Brueggemann, *The Prophetic Imagination* (Minneapolis: Fortress Press, 2001), 41–42.

2. Ibid, 45.

3. In the parallel passage for this scripture in the Gospel of Luke (9:23) Jesus says, "Deny your self, take up your cross *daily*," emphasizing the ongoing nature of the minister's conversion journey.

The Community Remembers and Re-Members

Eating the Words

4

You have a gift, and if you don't share it, you lose it. Remember, it's all about telling stories.

– Paul Neves,
Hula Master, Keaukaha, Hawaii

Each of us has stories embedded in our memories. Stories echo our past life experiences; they shape our future life experiences. Collectively, our stories create a vision of who we are—our fears, dreams, hopes, and yearnings. There are stories within us of childhood and family life, stories of coming of age, stories of travel and new friendships, stories of primary relationships—joyful and painful and ecstatic and tragic memories that are as much a part of us as our hands or lungs or nervous system. Some stories we choose to remember; other stories choose us and continue to resound in us, with or without our collaboration. Even stories that our conscious mind has suppressed live in and through us.

In my family, dead folk jumped in and out of conversations all the time.[1]

– Lizzy Walker

When I began to learn the Blessingway it changed my whole life. I began really thinking about ceremonies. I had heard singing before that but now I began to take it more seriously because I began to realize what life was and the kind of hardships we have to go through. Before I started learning Blessingway, the older people used to tell me that I should think about life more seriously. "If you don't know any songs you have nothing to go by. If a child grows up in a family like that he doesn't know where he is going or what he is doing." That is what the older people told me, that I should have something to live by.[2]

– Frank Mitchell,
Navajo Blessingway Singer

Beyond our individual and family stories are the larger stories of our ethnic groups, our national identities, and our religious beliefs. These stories form the backdrop to our individual stories. They anchor us and give us a perspective beyond ourselves. They offer hope when our individual stories cause us to despair, and they help us see the connection between our stories and the stories of others. Through them, we are called beyond our own narrow interests to a larger and deeper vision of life and goodness and truth. When we forget our stories, we quickly lose our way.

The Hebrew and Christian scriptures are such stories. They give us a view of reality that transcends shifting cultural values and the limitations of our own religious and secular institutions. In the scriptures, we come to know that the God who encounters us in the humanity of Jesus is large enough to encompass all times and places. The great stories of our tradition tell us that this God has been and continues to be incarnated and involved in the life of the world.

The great stories of our faith are essential for the formation and growth of the individual Christian and of the Christian community. They teach us again and again that our God is ever loving, ever present, and ever active in the world. When these stories are proclaimed with strength and conviction in our liturgies, and when assemblies hear them with understanding and openness, God's Spirit is able to shape, encourage, and renew us as individuals and as a community of faith.

REAPPROPRIATING OUR MEMORIES

Given the central role that these stories play in our faith life, consider this assertion by theologian Walter Brueggemann:

> The contemporary American church is so largely enculturated to the American ethos of consumerism that it has little power to believe or to act. . . The internal cause of such enculturation is our loss of identity through the abandonment of the faith tradition. *Our consumer culture is organized against history. There is a depreciation of memory and a ridicule of hope*, which means everything must be held in the now, either an urgent now or an eternal now... *The church has no business more pressing than the reappropriation of its memory in its full power and authenticity.*[3]

Brueggemann suggests that the American Church is in a state of amnesia. It has abandoned its faith tradition and its living memory and has lost its fundamental identity. The strong and deep understanding of the Church's call and mission has been replaced by an "ethos of consumerism" that has no appreciation of the past or vision of the future, but seeks only immediate gratification and consumption. From such a cultural perspective, the great stories cease to have meaning or power to shape and nurture the community. They can no longer challenge our beliefs and practices and fire our renewal and transformation into people of the Word.

If this is true, a great responsibility falls on those who lead the community in its worship—we who choose, write, and proclaim most of the words that the community will hear, speak, and/or sing. But that is not enough. We must also be responsible for how those words are heard and for *how* the community is invited into responding.

All too often our experience of worship does not involve the powerful and passionate proclamation of the Word through speech and song. The words of prayer or song or intercession are too often haphazardly crafted or chosen and too poorly presented to bring forth a response of joy and gratitude.

A friend from Ghana once described to me how the true artists in his country were those who knew the stories (memories) of the people, knew the relationships (community dynamics) of the people, and understood the vision (faith) of the people. When a member of the community felt fragmented or separated from the community he or she would go to the artist, who would sing the faith stories and "re-member" him or her back into the community.[4]

Our communities will never hear and recognize the great faith stories as their own or embrace them as the transforming call of God unless lectors, presiders, cantors, choir directors, and music ensembles embody the passion and urgency of those stories in their ministries. We must develop a deep and true understanding of these stories and of the individuals and communities who first lived and told them. We must feed ourselves and our ministries on study and prayer. Once we have "eaten the Word" and made it our own, we will come to understand how this Word—these stories—interact with, support, and challenge the contemporary stories of our community and its members. When the great stories of the tradition and the stories of today speak to each other, the Word becomes flesh yet again, full of grace and hope.

THE ROLE OF THE ASSEMBLY

When ministers forget the primary and crucial role of the assembly in the proclamation of these stories, the people's vision falters. When the members of our community do not perceive their response to be needed or wanted, they soon become passive. They will not respond, and soon they will cease to be attentive. They will not hear the stories because they will not understand that they are their own stories.

A critical role (perhaps *the* critical role) of all liturgical ministers is to help their community know itself through the remembering and retelling of the great faith stories. This means that we must keep those stories fresh and alive in ourselves.

The highlands that straddle the border between Laos and Cambodia are the ancestral home of the Hmong people. Until recently, the Hmong had no written language, and, consequently, no written literature. When missionaries made contact with the Hmong people they heard rich stories of the people's history, myths, and visions. "It is too bad," said the missionaries to the Hmong, "that you do not have a written language. You could write these stories down in books and preserve them." "We used to have books," the Hmong replied, "until one day we were cooking and the books fell in the rice and we ate them." After determining that they heard correctly, the missionaries expressed sympathy that the Hmong had lost their books. "Oh, no," was the answer. "Now that we have eaten the words, the stories are inside of us and we can tell them to you." [5]

This is not about some abstract or spiritualized knowing of the scriptures. If these words within the Word are truly central to our own faith and the faith formation of our communities, we presiders, lectors, and cantors will commit ourselves to doing the work of making these words our own—to eat them. Why should we expect the members of our congregations to take the Word home in their hearts if the ministers who read and sing them barely seem know or care about what they proclaim? We who minister must care enough about the Word of God to know it so well that it speaks from our hearts to the hearts of those in our communities. In this way, we help the "Word become flesh" anew.

This discovery...[the written alphabet] will create forgetfulness in the learners' souls, because they will not use their memories, they will trust to the external written characters and not remember of themselves...[It] is an aid not to memory but to recollection, and gives...only the semblance of truth; they will hear much and learn nothing; they will appear to know much and will generally know nothing...They will seem wise without being wise.

– Socrates

What would be the effect on our congregations (and on us) if each week the lector, the cantor, the choir, and the preacher all knew the readings and the psalm well enough to direct their focus off the page and toward the assembly as they proclaimed and sang a message that had become part of their own prayer lives?

The ministry of Jesus provides us with a strong and clear model for how the minister must connect to the great faith stories. The deep and abiding way that he knew scriptures is the way that we must seek to know them if we are to be faithful to our calling. This way of knowing is more than simply repeating or memorizing words; it is living with the stories, coming to know the people behind them, coming to know the God they encountered, and coming to perceive that their stories are our stories.

For Jesus, the teachings and stories of Hebrew scriptures were the constant anchor for his prophetic teaching and healing. He knew the scriptures well enough to quote them from memory.[6] However, his knowledge went far beyond simply being able to repeat verses. Jesus had a deep and living connection to the Word of God and its meaning for the people who first shared and lived its stories. This profound relationship with the scriptures empowered him to speak prophetically in his own place and time—to critique and challenge the religious and cultural attitudes and practices of his day.

If our faith stories are to be relevant for our communities today, the liturgical ministers of the Word—presider, deacon, lector, cantor, schola, and/or choir—must play crucial roles. They must do much more than simply read or sing the text; they must proclaim the Word—announce and embody its life and relevance to the worshiping community. To do this with integrity, they must first have "eaten" the words themselves.

[The Lord said to Ezekiel,] "You shall speak my words to [the people of Israel], whether they hear or refuse to hear; for they are a rebellious house. But you, mortal, hear what I say to you; do not be rebellious like that rebellious house; open your mouth and eat what I give you." I looked, and a hand was stretched out to me, and a written scroll was in it. He spread it before me; it had writing on the front and on the back, and written on it were words of lamentation and mourning and woe.

– Ezekiel 2:7–10

Throughout the history of Judaism and Christianity, prophets have been those who ate the Word, who made it their own. Jesus knew that his followers would need a profound knowledge of scripture as a primary tool for their ministry. He understood that God's Word provides a critical role in helping the community remember who they are. In Matthew, he says to his disciples, "Therefore every scribe who has been trained for the kingdom of heaven is like the master of a household who brings out of his treasure what is new and what is old" (Matthew 3:52). While the Word of God as handed down in our tradition is a very old treasure, the minister's insight and understanding make it a new and relevant treasure.

MUSIC, MEMORY, AND THE GREAT STORIES

Think of the songs you know from memory. What are they about? This is no idle question, because the songs we hold in memory, the songs that have truly become a part of us, have a power to shape our beliefs and actions. As Matthew Arnold writes, "We become what we sing."

What we sing, over time, we come to remember. What we remember, over time, we come to believe. What we believe, over time, we come to live. So think again about the songs you know from memory. Are they television theme songs (from *Friends* or *Gilligan's Island*), commercial jingles ("It's the real thing"), or songs from childhood or your formative years?

The music minister is a minister of the Word every bit as much as a lector, deacon, or presider. Indeed, music is in many ways the most powerful vehicle for passing on the stories of faith. For good or ill, music (especially the words of our hymns and songs) plays a critical role in defining the community's identity and vision. While most North American Roman Catholics could not recite even a few verses of Psalm 91 from memory, many could sing several verses of "On Eagle's Wings" without the printed music. The same could be said for many Lutherans of Psalm 46 and "A Mighty Fortress" or of most Christians regarding Psalm 96 and "Joy to the World." The fact that the words of our songs remain embedded in our assembly's consciousness long after the music has died away should give each music minister pause.

A few years back, I presented a workshop to a small parish in the Big Island of Hawaii. The pastor told me that he had used my setting of Psalm 23, "Shepherd Me, O God," each week for the entire Lenten season. During the third week of Easter, he heard young school children singing the song from memory on the playground. They had eaten the psalm, and now it belonged to them.

THE STORIES WE LOVE AND THE WORDS WE CANNOT SWALLOW

The profession of journalism should be about telling people what they need to know rather than what they want to know.[7]

– Walter Cronkite

Chapter Three of this book focuses on how continuous conversion is at the heart of the Christian journey. When we honestly face the stories of our scriptures, they call us again and again beyond our areas of comfort. Both Roman Catholic and many Protestant denominations have organized the reading of scripture on Sunday in a way that enables us over a three-year cycle to hear a broad and rich selection of the most central stories and writings of our faith.

When we live and pray faithfully with the Lectionary, we are able to call upon a deep and living source that can feed and challenge any community. Through the seasons and celebrations of the church year, we hear praise and petition, rejoicing and lament, joy and deep sorrow. The musician who spends time with these texts, prays with them, and makes musical choices that support and illumine them provides the assembly with a voice that can rejoice in times of blessing, lament in times of sorrow, and seek renewal and healing in times of forgetfulness and brokenness.

At times, scripture will speak in words that are difficult for a community to swallow. The role of the minister in these times—preacher, reader, musician—is to proclaim those words bravely to the community and challenge them to echo the words back. The prophetic Word often uncovers and names our own injustice and unfaithfulness. We must sing these words honestly and clearly if we are to be faithful to our calling.

HEAD WORK: LEARNING THE STORIES

Do your homework. It is ironic that many parish musicians sing scriptural songs, psalms, and canticles each week with very little understanding of the Word itself. If we are called to proclaim the Word, in word or song, it is not enough to read or sing through it "just enough to get by." If we truly want to connect the Word with the real life experiences of our own community, then we must have some understanding of the life experiences of the people within the stories—their hopes and fears, their beliefs and doubts, and, most of all, their experience of God at work in their lives. We need to know something of the background of the writer, the community the story was written for, and the historical setting in which it was written. This can only be obtained by spending time with the reading, as well as with commentaries and worship preparation aids that help us get the context of the reading. This kind of study is important for all those involved in liturgy preparation—musicians and non-musicians, lay and ordained ministers.

HEART WORK: LOVING THE STORIES

Come to know and love the stories of faith.

We cannot ask anyone in our congregations to take the Word home in his or her heart if we have not first lived with it in our own hearts. All of us who proclaim the Word through speech or song need to spend time each week reading and sharing and praying that word. Group rehearsal times are critical for all the group members to hear the Word for the coming week, share their reflections, and pray over the text.

When Joe Camacho was the music director at Malia, Puka O'Kalani (Mary, Gate of Heaven) parish in Hilo, Hawaii, he gathered the cantors once a week. Joe would teach the music for the next several weeks to all cantors at once, so they would know it well. But before he taught the music, the entire group looked at the readings for the coming week, reflected upon their meaning, and shared how those readings affected their own lives. Sometimes this period took much of the rehearsal time, yet Joe felt the time together with the Word was critical for their effectiveness as ministers.

Come to know and love the stories of the community.

Our faith stories do not exist only in the past. If they did, they would have no power to liberate and save us. The stories of our faith must be alive and true here and now. This means they must be living within and through the stories of our community. If this is to happen, all ministers have the responsibility of knowing the community with which they pray—their stories, their joys and sorrows, their moments of strength and weakness. Only then can they help the community understand that the ancient story is truly alive within their midst this very day.

HANDIWORK: EATING THE WORDS

Help your ministry learn to eat the words.

Christian faith formation always involves common support. Assign someone from your ministry to come to each week's rehearsal prepared not only to proclaim a reading for the coming week, but also to offer a brief reflection and invite the group to pray in the spirit of the reading. If you are the one who chooses the music, make it clear to the group how your choices were intended to support and strengthen the spoken Word. (You do make the choices that way, don't you?)

Help the community to craft new chapters in their stories.

The primary role of any minister is to help the community connect the great stories of faith with their own stories, so that the Gospel of Jesus is their song and the Word is living within them. Create rituals that allow the stories to manifest themselves physically in your midst. One parish delayed entering their new worship space until the night of the great Easter Vigil. Processing past the Paschal candle and the font into the church for the first time, most of the members of the congregation were in tears. Years later, the "Alleluia" they sang at that moment still shapes their understanding of their new life in Christ.

---

1. Quoted in Lisa Evans, *Stamping, Shouting and Singing Home.*
2. Charlotte J. Frisbie and David P. McAllester. *Navajo Blessingway Singer: Frank Mitchell 1881–1967* (Tucson: University of Arizona Press, 1978).
3. Walter Brueggemann, *Prophetic Imagination* (Philadelphia: Fortress Press, 1978). 11–12. Emphasis added.
4. From a conversation with ethnomusicologist Sowah Mensah.
5. Related by Pia Moriarty, teacher and anthropologist.
6. See Matthew 4:4–10; 7:10; 21:13; 26:31; Mark 7:6; Luke 18:31; 21:22–23; 22:37; 24:27, 46; John 6:45; 8:17; 10:34.
7. From a television interview on the *Today* show (NBC), August 9, 2001.

The Perilous Invitation
of the Gospel

To say yes is to make a leap of faith, to risk oneself in a new and often scary relationship. Not being quite sure of what we are doing, or where it will lead us, we try on assent, we commit ourselves to affirmation.[1]

– Kathleen Norris

Christianity is a profoundly relational religion. The quality and nature of our own relationship with God is mirrored and manifested, nurtured and expressed through our relationships with one another. When we proclaim that God became one of us, we also proclaim that God is present in every person we encounter—friend and enemy, stranger and loved one. The way that we build faithful, compassionate relationships or the way that we abuse and hurt each other cannot be separated from our relationship with God.

Those who say, "I love God," and hate their brothers or sisters, are liars; for those who do not love a brother or sister whom they have seen, cannot love God whom they have not seen. The commandment we have from him is this: those who love God must love their brothers and sisters also.

– 1 John 4:20–21

The apostle Paul wrote to the fledgling Christian community at Corinth about the minister's calling:

If I proclaim the gospel, this gives me no ground for boasting, for an obligation is laid on me, and woe to me if I do not proclaim the gospel! For if I do this of my own will, I have a reward; but if not of my own will, I am entrusted with a commission...For though I am free with respect to all, *I have made myself a slave to all,* so that I might win more of them. To the Jews I became as a Jew, in

59

order to win Jews. To those under the law I became as one under the law (though I myself am not under the law) so that I might win those under the law. To those outside the law I became as one outside the law (though I am not free from God's law but am under Christ's law) so that I might win those outside the law. To the weak I became weak, so that I might win the weak. I have become all things to all people, that I might by all means save some. I do it all for the sake of the gospel, so that I may share in its blessings (1 Corinthians 9:16–17, 19–23).

The call of every Christian, like Paul's, is to become "a slave to all" so that others might say "yes" to God's call. In this model of ministry, power is given over to the one being ministered to, and the minister becomes the more vulnerable person. This is a radically different model from that of the performer or the professional who sings or speaks or acts from a position of power and authority. Think of the trappings of the entertainer—the hand-held microphone, the attentive audience, a special focal point from which to sing or speak. Think of our contemporary culture, which almost deifies musical performers and TV newscasters. To keep a clear vision of our role of servant minister in such an environment is difficult.

The subtle but critical difference between a pseudo-ministry focused on oneself and a genuine ministry focused on the other is lived out in the dynamic of invitation and response. All true ministry is an invitation to others to respond to the Gospel. In a genuine invitation, the one who invites becomes vulnerable, because a genuine invitation (as opposed to manipulation or coercion) leaves the listener with the option of saying no.

The extent of the minister's vulnerability increases with the depth of the invitation. In moments of profound relational change (think about the first time "I love you" is spoken in a new relationship), the one who invites becomes very vulnerable. It is tempting for the minister to hide within the role of performer or entertainer because the performer does not have to risk the rejection of his or her invitation. Even more frightening, perhaps, is that the one who has been invited may accept; then the minister must enter into a deeper and mutually life-changing relationship.

Peter began to say to him, "Look, we have left everything and followed you." Jesus said, "Truly I tell you, there is no one who has left house or brothers or sisters or mother or father or children or fields, for my sake and for the sake of the good news, who will not receive a hundredfold now in this age—houses, brothers and sisters, mothers and children, and fields with persecutions—and in the age to come eternal life. But many who are first will be last, and the last will be first."

– Mark 10:28–31

It is easy to think of Jesus as the greatest success story of all time, but when we look carefully at the Gospels we realize that many times people said no to his invitation. Although the Gospels mention that at various times great crowds followed Jesus, at his death only a tiny band was present. Those who followed him, including most of his closest disciples, could not accept the radical challenge of his invitation of service even unto death.

Within liturgy, the minister's task is to invite all present into a deeper and more authentic common faith journey. The Gospel that we proclaim celebrates a God intimately present among us when we gather to sing, pray, talk, and share an ever-growing faith relationship with one another.

Leading people in song or prayer or proclaiming the Word within liturgy can be frightening or disconcerting for many people. There is the obvious fear of making a mistake in front of others, but there is another fearful element at work. The minister who has been called into discipleship is inevitably called to invite others to discipleship as well. When Christian ministry is taken seriously, it quickly moves beyond singing songs or reading the text or giving out communion. If we "become a slave to all," we use all our skills and every opportunity to be at the service of others. It often will mean reexamining the way we make music, speak, and serve, asking ourselves hard questions about our motives and methods of ministry.

Members of the music ensemble at a suburban church noticed that an elderly woman was often seen waiting at the door of the church for some time after liturgy. When they approached her, she told them that she depended on a public-ride program, which was often late and sometimes unable to transport her. In response, the music group adopted her; the members coordinated her trips to and from church. Later, they began to include her in their social gatherings as well. They understood that real ministry grew beyond making music "for" others into a deeper commitment and relationship "with" others.

– Bonnie Faber, music minister
Minneapolis, Minnesota

Liturgical ministers, especially those in larger parishes, can easily find ways to avoid real, meaningful contact with members of the parish and the occasional stranger who may show up. But if we succumb to this temptation, we have chosen not the hard path of the servant but the easy path of the performer.

The importance of invitation and response within the liturgical experience does not mean that the minister can escape from the hard work of developing musical and public communication skills. The minister values these skills all the more because of his or her call or, as Paul says, because of the "obligation laid on" and the "commission" entrusted to him or her. But for the minister, all these skills (as well as all the trappings of ministry) are used not for self-glorification or career advancement, but "for the sake of the Gospel" and in order to bring others to that Gospel.

THE HARD ROAD OF INVITATION

If you have watched a televised football game in the United States sometime in the past two decades, you have probably seen someone in the end zone holding up a sign that reads "John 3:16." This passage, "For God so loved the world that he gave his only Son, so that everyone who believes in him may not perish but may have eternal life," is a source of strength and comfort for many Christians. It is interesting, however, that no one ever holds up a sign that reads "Mark 8:34": "[Jesus] called the crowd with his disciples, and said to them, 'If any want to become my followers, let them deny themselves and take up their cross and follow me.'"

Although just as true as John 3:16, the passage from Mark is much less popular. We like to remember that God's love is boundless and relies only on our belief, while we tend to avoid the text in which Jesus calls us to deny ourselves and take up our cross. For those of us who minister, it is difficult in at least two ways.

First, we cannot honestly ask our communities to "deny themselves" until we ourselves have answered Jesus' invitation to discipleship. Liturgical ministers (especially presiders, deacons, musicians, and lectors) sometimes seem more interested in calling attention to themselves than in denying themselves. Second, many ministers believe, with some justification, that people will reject such a challenging invitation. Here is a reading from the Gospel of Mark:

> As he was setting out on a journey, a man ran up and knelt before him, and asked him, "Good Teacher, what must I do to inherit eternal life?" Jesus said to him, "Why do you call me good? No one is good but God alone. You know the commandments: 'You shall not murder; You shall not commit adultery; You shall not steal; You shall not bear false witness; You shall not defraud; Honor your father and mother.'" He said to him, "Teacher, I have kept all these since my youth." Jesus, looking at him, loved him and said, "You lack one thing; go, sell what you own, and give the money to the poor, and you will have treasure in heaven; then come, follow me." When he heard this, he was shocked and went away grieving, for he had many possessions (Mark 10:17–22).

The rich man in the story was at the center, the position of strength. He knew the Jewish commandments and practiced them faithfully. His many possessions would give him acceptability within his society. He would have been the sort of person we would love to have on our parish council or in our choir or praise band. Yet Jesus challenges and invites him to a deeper, more difficult way. The invitation is so clear and strong that it cannot be ignored. The man could say "yes" or "no," but he could not pretend that he had not been invited.

Then Jesus looked around and said to his disciples, "How hard it will be for those who have wealth to enter the kingdom of God!" And the disciples were perplexed at these words. But Jesus said to them again, "Children, how hard it is to enter the kingdom of God! It is easier for a camel to go through the eye of a needle than for someone who is rich to enter the kingdom of God." They were greatly astounded and said to one another,

"Then who can be saved?" Jesus looked at them and said, "For mortals it is impossible, but not for God; for God all things are possible."

— Mark 10:23–27

How deep and challenging is this invitation that we are called to first accept and then pass on! We hear the amazement of Jesus' disciples when they exclaim, "Then who can be saved?" Jesus will not put a limit on the call of the disciple, yet he does make it clear that his life-changing call has its own reward, a reward that is radically different from the rewards that society offers.

The invitation made by the minister changes both the one inviting and the one invited, whether the invitation is accepted or not. If our invitation is rejected, we have still grown through the process, because we have opened ourselves to life and the possibility of sacramental relationship. The person who receives an invitation must choose and in the process is confronted by the same dilemma as the rich man Jesus invited.

As ministers, we are caught in a terrible bind. If our invitation is rejected, we run the risk of looking foolish. If it is accepted, we have yoked our journey to the one we have invited, and our own journey takes on a new and more challenging dimension. But in the end, ministers have no choice. As followers of Jesus, our ministry demands that we offer to others the same genuine and challenging invitation that we have received.

HEAD WORK: UNDERSTANDING OUR CONNECTION IN CHRIST

Consider how invitation happens or doesn't happen within your own worship experience.

Engaged and vibrant Christian communities do not happen by accident. A multitude of factors determine how community prayer invites, engages, and transforms assemblies. The careful formation of ministers and ministries, the quality of preparation and rehearsal, the physical space and arrangement of people within it, and the skills of the various ministries all play their parts. Ask yourself how inviting your community is to strangers, especially to those of a different social class or ethnic group from the majority of parishioners—gays and lesbians, single parents, the homeless, the mentally ill, and the developmentally or physically challenged. Then consider your particular ministry: Is your music group (lector group, hospitality ministry) open and inviting? Do its members welcome others to join?

Learn the skills of invitation.

For those in leadership positions within worship, communication skills are absolutely critical. These skills, like all of our talents, should not call attention to us; they are to be placed at the service of the community's prayer. We must be good communicators so that others experience a strong and clear invitation to join in a common, relational faith journey with us. Cantors need to know how and when to use gesture in a manner that gives helpful and hospitable invitation without appearing condescending, manipulative, or self-centered. All ministers of the Word must live with the readings and prayers so deeply that in their proclamation only the Word is heard, not the speaker. We must develop our own particular gifts—in music, spoken word, dance, and hospitality—so that the assembled know that they have received a clear and inspiring invitation into the prayer.

Learn to lead as servant.

The truth is that sometimes we are more focused on our own performance or the performance of our choir or ensemble than on the assembly's enthusiastic response. By continually reminding ourselves that we are servants to the assembly's prayer, we are more likely to lead as ministers than simply entertain as performers.

HEART WORK: EMBRACING OUR CONNECTION IN CHRIST

Be attentive and open to others.

Because the heart of ministry is service, we cannot be effective ministers unless we are willing to be vulnerable to others, empathetic and responsive to their needs. This does not mean that we simply wallow in the pain of others; it does mean that we always remember that Christ is present to us in those whom we serve (see Matthew 25:34–40) both within and outside of our communities.

Widen your circle of invitation.

Look for opportunities in your neighborhood, school, and workplace to make new friendships that broaden your life beyond your comfort zone. Learn to see differences with others as an opportunity to grow in understanding and wisdom as you listen and come to know them.

HANDIWORK: DEVELOPING THE CRAFT OF COMMUNICATION AND INVITATION

Understanding the importance of the minister's invitation and making the choice to be inviting are not enough. The effective Christian minister needs to develop the very practical skills of communication, public leadership, song leading and effective proclamation of the Word. The Bibliography at the end of this book offers a number of publications that contain guidance for the liturgical minister. Here are some very simple and practical suggestions:

Know the Word that you proclaim, the prayers and songs you lead.

The more that we have internalized the Word, psalms, hymns, and prayer before prayer begins, the better able we are to focus on those in our assembly. Then we are able to invite with confidence, letting the power of the Word within us speak through us.

Keep your focus on the assembly.

Once you have internalized and owned the words that you must sing, proclaim, and pray, train yourself to lift your eyes from the music or scripture and look into the eyes of those with whom you pray. Offer gestures that are simple and clear, with only as much direction as needed. Let the size of the space, the size of the congregation, and your visibility dictate your gestures. Never demean the congregation by engaging in unneeded gestures or conducting.

Practice listening skills in liturgy.

Be present to sound in all its forms within the worship space, trying to experience the sacred in sound's presence. Try especially to listen—really listen—to the sound of the assembly when they sing. If you can't hear them, make your own voice quieter. If you still can't hear them, ask yourself why not. Is it the acoustics, the repertoire, weak leadership, or poor accompaniment?

Use the rehearsal time before prayer to engage and invite the assembly.

A simple and hospitable rehearsal before liturgy begins allows the music minister to invite the assembly into a relational and collaborative prayer experience. Teach music in simple and short lines, listen carefully to the congregation's response, and then bolster their confidence with praise. Offer short and relevant background about the text, the culture that created it, or the use of the music within the prayer so that the community understands what they are singing and why.

Videotape the ministers during liturgy.

Videotape all the ministers, starting with yourself. Invite them to watch the videos in small groups to offer loving critique. Ask everyone to consider whether they would feel welcomed and supported to respond as members of the congregation.

Continue to develop your skills.

Simply singing, speaking, or praying does not make us effective song leaders, proclaimers of the Word, or presiders. Take every opportunity for continuing education, even it means traveling to workshops and conferences some distance from your home. Although videos and books can help, there is no substitute for working and learning in the presence of good teachers and mentors. Try to get a budget from your parish to assist a number of ministers in continuing education opportunities.

---

1. Kathleen Norris, *Amazing Grace: A Vocabulary of Faith* (New York: Riverhead Books, 1998).

THE SACRED MEAL:
SHARING THE FEAST OF LIFE

Living Tradition and Living Culture

6

Then the Pharisees and scribes came to Jesus from Jerusalem and said, "Why do your disciples break the tradition of the elders? For they do not wash their hands before they eat." He answered them, "And why do you break the commandment of God for the sake of your tradition?"

– Matthew 15:1–3

The Chinese have a saying: "May you live in interesting times." This saying is meant as a curse, not a blessing. In these early years of a new millennium, radical and sweeping changes taking place in the worship of North American Christians (and the passionate discussions around those changes) have indeed created such "interesting times."

Those who prepare and lead Christian community prayer find themselves caught up in situations in which the form, language, music, focus, and style of worship often become battlegrounds for various parish factions. Some individuals and communities cling to a particular tradition of worship and reject the introduction of new elements or practices. Others label much or all of a particular worship tradition as meaningless or irrelevant and seek to fashion a worship life that resembles the familiar elements of the secular culture found in concerts, plays, or television. Many churches find themselves caught between the two perspectives, trying somehow to honor and hold both tradition and cultural relevance. They try to combine traditional and cultural elements within the same celebration, or they provide multiple parish celebrations, each expressing a different flavor of worship.

The variety of terminology used in regard to worship in various communities is a good indicator of the complexity of the problem. "Traditional," "contemporary," "blended," "praise," "youth," "alternative," or "family" worship—these labels mean very different things to different people, and they often carry strong positive or negative connotations, depending on the bias of the person speaking or listening to the discussion. At a denominational level, many churches struggle to find a core worship tradition or repertoire that all their member churches will embrace.

The question of preserving, adapting, or abandoning a worship tradition is vital because, more than any other event, worship names, defines, forms, and reflects Christian community. The words we pray, proclaim, and sing and the actions we do have tremendous power to form and direct our understanding of our relationship to God, to one another, and to all of life. When we make changes in the content and form of our worship, it is essential that we act with wisdom and perspective. True renewal seeks a way of worship that is faithful to the living tradition handed down from Christians through the centuries while expressing our experience of that same faith in this time and place. It can't be achieved easily or quickly.

Worship renewal can be understood as getting back to the authentic roots of Christian community prayer. It is not about creating something completely new; rather, it means rediscovering, reenvisioning, and rearticulating something very old that is eternally living and true. Bishop Donald Trautman, the former chair of the United States Catholic Bishops' Committee on the Liturgy, defines *tradition* as something that is at the heart of living and faithful Christian prayer (apart from a particular cultural expression), as opposed to *traditional*, the expression of a particular culture, which must continually be evaluated in the light of tradition.[1]

THE TRADITION OF JESUS AND THE EARLY CHURCH

When we examine the life of Jesus as we receive it from the scriptures, it is clear that he was faithful to his own Jewish religious tradition.

> Do not think that I have come to abolish the law or the prophets; I have come not to abolish but to fulfill. For truly I tell you, until heaven and earth pass away, not one letter, not one stroke of a letter, will pass from the law until all is accomplished...Unless your righteousness exceeds that of the scribes and Pharisees, you will never enter the kingdom of heaven (Matthew 5:17–18, 20).

Jesus' radical faithfulness caused him to challenge the religious leaders of his time to keep their tradition alive and engaged in the world. He understood the critical importance of religious tradition in keeping the individual and the community faithful to God's law. He also understood, however, that God's law existed for the benefit and salvation of all people, especially the most vulnerable. His harshest criticism was reserved for those who used religious tradition as an excuse to act without compassion (Matthew 12:1–8; 15:1–14). Jesus never lost sight of the truth that religious traditions are established to help all people recognize, praise, love, and serve God in a way that brings joy and meaning to life.

From the very beginning, Christian worship reflected the creative tension between an established religious tradition and the various cultures into which that tradition was introduced. The first Christians followed the Jewish religious practices that Jesus observed—Temple worship, synagogue attendance, and sacred meal rituals (Acts 2:46; 3:1; 14:1; 17:1–2; 24:11–12). But within a matter of a few decades, as communities sprang up across the Middle East and Southern Europe, Christian worship began to incorporate, reflect, and respond to elements and attitudes from the surrounding cultures, including Roman, Greek, and Syrian influences. Throughout the centuries, Christian worship has continued to reflect the struggle between tradition and culture.

People were not created to serve liturgical traditions. As Jesus told some religious people of his day, "The Sabbath was made for humankind, and not humankind for the Sabbath" (Mark 2:27). Christian liturgical traditions arose from the community's acts of thanksgiving, praise, and petition to God; they became tradition because they were found to help reveal and celebrate God's presence.

Not everything that arises from the community becomes tradition; not every tradition continues to reveal and celebrate God's presence in every time and place. This does not mean that we take our worship traditions lightly—changing them, dropping them, or adding to them without thought or awareness.[2] Our traditions serve us well when they connect us to the fullness of the Gospel—to the God we proclaim, to the faithful who have gone before us, and to the Christian's life in the world. Any change must be tested against that measure.

CREATIVE TENSION AND THE SPIRIT'S PRESENCE

It is natural for humans to try to avoid situations that create tension, but tension is inherent in all human life, including the life of the Christian community. Those of us who prepare and lead worship are painfully aware that "where two or three are gathered in my name, I am there among them" and there's going to be a fight over the liturgy. As unpleasant as such tension may be, creative tension is essential to achieving growth. God's Spirit moves most powerfully through chaos—over the waters of Creation, in the storm of Good Friday, in the wind and fire of Pentecost in Jerusalem. We should try to remain open to the possibility that God's Spirit can move within and through our personal and professional difficulties to "renew the face of the earth," for us and for those with whom we work.

One of the great sources of tension in church life is the fact that we are part of a living—which means ever-changing—tradition. A living tradition will inevitably develop over time, because it will continually be called upon to express the truth of the eternal God's action within time, and our confident hope in God's action in the present and future. Worship must be attuned to this creative tension between our past, our world today, and our vision of God's reign. We must develop the perspective and courage to choose music and texts that offer both praise and lament, both comfort and challenge. We must balance songs that express awe and wonder toward the transcendent God of all eternity with songs that express and praise the often challenging and countercultural actions of an immanent God in our world, here and now. We must present music and prayers that speak and inspire our particular community, while reflecting a God who speaks to and through the people of every culture and every time.

Many Christians, especially those raised within a liturgical tradition with a familiar body of music, strongly resist any changes to the texts, music, actions, and prayers they learned during their formative years. Their resistance is an important reminder to be cautious in making changes and careful to preserve the treasures of our heritage. It reminds us that before we critique and attempt to change a tradition, we must thoroughly understand and respect its history and our own place in it. At the same time, new music and texts, especially those from Christians of other cultures, provide us with additional lenses through which to view community prayer. They also give us a wider perspective that enables us to better critique the usefulness and meaning of all liturgical music and ritual action, old and new.

Those who choose the music for community prayer have a tremendous responsibility. The words we put in the mouths of our congregations (and eventually, in their memories and hearts) will become the theology that shapes their faith. The way that they are invited and supported—or not invited and supported—to participate in the music making at worship will profoundly form their understanding of the relationships within community and play a major part in shaping their sense of involvement or non-involvement in the prayer.

But the experience of community prayer is much more than music. It includes everything that we say and do. One of the most formative aspects of prayer is how we relate to one another through our words and actions. Who is recognized as first and who as last? How do our words and actions unite us, and how do they manifest and reinforce divisions?

It is critical that those who lead the community in worship have a deep and vital understanding of their worship tradition. But oftentimes those of us in ministry—both volunteer and paid—find ourselves in positions of responsibility with little background in the history or meaning of the liturgy. That may simply be a result of the path that brought us to this ministry, but it must be addressed. If we are asked to select the music and prepare the liturgy for our communities, let us use the opportunity to educate ourselves about the history and meaning of our community prayer.[3] If we truly care about the quality and extent of our community's involvement in liturgy, we must begin by educating ourselves in the meaning and shape of the Eucharist.

We cannot intelligently change or renew any tradition that we do not thoroughly understand; we cannot be faithful in our renewal unless our changes are grounded in a deep and abiding love for the original intent and expression of the ritual. Developing this genuine understanding of our tradition is our "head" work; developing openness to how we can embrace an ever-growing and more diverse living tradition is our "heart" work; building a strong and deep and broad community involvement in the integrity and power of worship planning is critical "handiwork."

HEAD WORK: LEARNING THE TRADITION

A person can love the rhythm, beauty, and power of a liturgical tradition without understanding all of its history and evolution. But this affection for the tradition is not enough for those of us who plan liturgy, who help to form communities in their own understanding, those who choose music, and those who lead communities in sung and spoken word from week to week and season to season.

Learn the history of the liturgy.

A river only remains strong, clear, and alive while it continues to be fed from its source and from the many streams that flow into it. Christian worship must stay connected to the living tradition, to the many fresh and life-giving streams of cultures and traditions that have nourished it. Ministers, paid or volunteer, leader or group member, must continually immerse themselves in this living river if their ministry is to be faithful. Fortunately, there are many excellent resources that can provide every minister with an excellent foundation in liturgical tradition. Many of them are listed in the Bibliography at the end of the book.

Seek out opportunities for additional education.

This does not mean that every music minister and lector and liturgist has to undertake a formal degree program (although leaders of ministries should aspire toward such training). Call your diocesan or synod office of worship, and make sure that you get all information about coming events that focus on the liturgical ministries. Get a membership for the music director, clergy, deacon, and anyone else you can in organizations such as the National Association of Pastoral Musicians (NPM), the American Guild of Organists (AGO), or the Association of Lutheran Church Musicians (ALCM). Find ways to get funds from your parish to send as many people as possible to workshops and conferences. It is a small price for a parish to pay, given the central importance of worship in shaping the community life.

HEART WORK: EMBRACING GOD'S BIG TENT

Be open to the Spirit's movement.

While we may believe that we know the best way to prepare and lead worship, we must always be open to the possibility that the Spirit can speak through other people and their visions. Oftentimes, it is precisely when our best-laid plans seem to go wrong that God's grace breaks through, if only we are open to it.

Invite reaction and criticism from the community and other ministers.

The minister who believes that he or she is the "liturgical expert" in the community who passes on wisdom to the "ignorant" assembly has already effectively killed the possibility of growing in wisdom and vision. The Spirit of God resides in each of us, and everyone's voice must be welcomed, heard, and honored if our prayer is to be truly sacramental. Never forget that God speaks through all people, every culture, and all expressions. We must not shut ourselves off from the possibility of the presence of God's Spirit in any new experience.

HANDIWORK: FAITHFUL, PROPHETIC WORSHIP

Practice carefully pruning instead of clear-cutting.

Those who plan and prepare worship are often tempted, especially after attending a workshop or class on liturgy, to make sweeping or dramatic changes in parish worship with little preparation or thought about the community's history and attachment to the prayer. By careful preparation, judicious introduction of changes (letting people know about what will be changed and why), and genuine opportunities for reaction from community members, the chance of a parish community embracing change is much higher.

Don't leave any ministers out of the education process.

There are small, informative books, such as *Music in Catholic Worship*, (see Bibliography) that are inexpensive enough when purchased in quantity that they could be provided for an entire music ministry (and make great Christmas gifts). Other excellent resources, like *The Mystery of Faith* (see Bibliography), may be studied together by a parish liturgy committee or an entire ensemble or choir. Without losing a great deal of practice time, the music director can talk to the ensemble or choir a bit each week about how and why choices are made in order to respect and renew the living tradition of Christian prayer.

Don't leave the community out of the education process.

Find ways to help your entire community better understand the history, meaning, and power of the liturgy. A column in the parish bulletin or newsletter, brief opportunities during pre-liturgy rehearsals, pamphlets explaining the worship elements and history available near the church entrance, and adult or family education sessions on liturgy can be very helpful in building community support and involvement in Sunday prayer.

Continually evaluate your worship.

Involve as wide a circle of community members as possible in opportunities in giving feedback about specific liturgies as well as seasons. The combination of careful education and open evaluation gives both music ministers and congregations a sense that their faith lives are respected and included.

---

1. From a talk given at the Los Angeles Diocesan Music Convention, October 27, 1995.
2. Pastor Dan Erlander says that before we can change elements at the heart of our liturgical tradition we have to have a "long conversation with the ancestors."
3. See the Bibliography for a selected list of resources on liturgical history, tradition, and structure.

The Marginalized as Host and Guest

7

As he sat at dinner in Levi's house, many tax collectors and sinners were also sitting with Jesus and his disciples—for there were many who followed him. When the scribes of the Pharisees saw that he was eating with sinners and tax collectors, they said to his disciples, "Why does he eat with tax collectors and sinners?" When Jesus heard this, he said to them, "Those who are well have no need of a physician, but those who are sick; I have come to call not the righteous but sinners."

— Mark 2:15–17

The urging I make to those who would be prophets is that we not neglect to do our work about who God is and that we know our discernment of God is at the breaking points of human community.[1]

— Walter Brueggemann

Ministry is never about business as usual. It is about our own part in the never-ending, ever-new Christian journey from the world as it is to the vision of God's reign of peace, justice, mercy, and equality. When we are in the midst of daily, practical tasks—preparing, studying, rehearsing, teaching, planning for parish events, leading a congregation in worship— it is natural for us to see the work that is immediately in front of us as an end in itself. We can come to believe that if we make good choices and play the music competently or proclaim the reading well, we have done all that we need to do.

Ministry that is focused upon itself, on its own accomplishments and skills and activities, is a dying ministry. Think of how often you have seen someone leading worship as a cantor, lector, presider, assisting minister, or choir member with his or her face totally absorbed in the music or text, barely aware of the people gathered. The same phenomena can happen in any area of ministry. Regardless of our particular gifts and tasks, we grow in our Christian ministry only when we look past our teaching, speaking, and musical skills and activities to invite, engage, and seek out those who are lonely, isolated, excluded, and absent from our community.

My brothers and sisters, do you with your acts of favoritism really believe in our glorious Lord Jesus Christ? For if a person with gold rings and in fine clothes comes into your assembly, and if a poor person in dirty clothes also comes in, and if you take notice of the one wearing the fine clothes and say, "Have a seat here, please," while to the one who is poor you say, "Stand there," or, "Sit at my feet," have you not made distinctions among yourselves, and become judges with evil thoughts? Listen, my beloved brothers and sisters. Has not God chosen the poor in the world to be rich in faith and to be heirs of the kingdom that he has promised to those who love him?

– James 2:1–5

Communities whose vision and energy end with their own programs and activities die. They may seem to be alive; they may even have large memberships, but if Christ's good news of service, healing, and nurturing to the poor, the weak, outsiders, and the vulnerable is not at the heart of all they do, they are little more than social clubs. Churches as a whole and Christians as individuals grow in faith only at the edge, at the margins—through the people who exist at the margins of community and society, and through the experiences that stretch and challenge us. Challenging people and challenging experiences allow the Spirit of God to draw us past our safe and familiar boundaries toward Christ's reign of mercy and peace and justice for all humanity, indeed for all of creation.

SUCCESSFUL MINISTRY

The life of Jesus teaches that it is precisely those at the very margins of our community and our society who should be our primary focus; it is precisely those experiences of the marginalized that become our greatest teachers. In the light of this perspective, how should we define "success" in our work as ministers?

In 1980, a Lutheran campus pastor counseled a student who was struggling to come to terms with his sexual identity. He was leaving school and felt he must also leave the church because he could not be gay and remain a practicing Christian. The pastor reassured him that the church exists precisely for those who feel themselves most alienated from and rejected by the world. Shortly after the young man left college, the pastor wrote him a note to encourage him in his faith.

Twenty years later, the man approached the pastor at a worship conference. He had stayed involved in the church and in active ministry. He showed the pastor the note she had written decades before. "I have kept this note in my box of treasures," he told her. "It has sustained me through all these years."

This is how success is measured in ministry—not by how well we attract large numbers of successful, happy people, but by how well we serve, nurture, heal, and empower the broken, ostracized, and rejected of the world. The reign that Jesus proclaimed was not primarily for the rich and proud and powerful (Matthew 19:23–24), but for the ones who were rejected by society (Mark 12:41–43; Luke 1:51–53).

In every society, in every time, people have been excluded, discriminated against, and even killed because of their ethnicity, social status, diseases, or personal behavior. The heart of the Jesus' message stands as witness on behalf of the weakest and most vulnerable (Matthew 11:2–5; Luke 4:16–21). Just as Jesus sought and welcomed the marginalized as first to share in the banquet of the reign of God (Luke 14:12–14), every follower of Jesus must follow his example, welcoming those whom the world would reject.

THE MARGINALIZED IN JESUS' SOCIETY

Who are the marginalized of our society today? Through an examination of the marginalized in Jesus' society, we can gain an understanding and sensitivity to those who suffer the same discrimination, isolation, neglect, and abuse in our midst. By looking at how Jesus expressed a radically just and loving image of God in his interaction with the marginalized of his time, we begin to understand our own calling in a new way.

Those afflicted with diseases carrying social or religious stigmas.

LEPERS: Until the twentieth century, those afflicted with leprosy bore not only a fatal and disfiguring disease but alienation as well. They were sent to live far from society, not welcome to return, and usually forgotten. In Jesus' time, lepers were considered ritually unclean, and no one would speak to them or have any contact with them.

In Matthew 8:1–4 the leper does not ask Jesus to be healed; he asks to be "made clean." For Jewish society in Jesus' day, to be clean meant being accepted as a full member of the community. Even more than being made physically whole, the leper is asking for acceptance from those who shunned him. In the version of this story found in Mark 1:40–45, Jesus is moved "with pity" or "deep emotion." The phrase could also be read "moved with anger"—Jesus rages against any religious teaching or practice that separates an individual, especially the weakest, from the support and love of the community. When Jesus says to the man, "Be made clean," the leprosy leaves him, and Jesus tells him to offer himself for the ritual cleansing. The healing of the leper's body was necessary so that the religious community would accept him, but Jesus had already welcomed him, touching him when others would not.

Like the lepers in Jesus' time, people in our world today who suffer from HIV infections and AIDS are often shunned far beyond the needed precautions to prevent contagion. They are isolated by the ignorance, fear, and prejudices of others. To the terrible cost of the disease is added a moral or religious judgment from those who would quickly and easily "cast the first stone." A few people, including some Christians, have even echoed the ancient attitude against illness from Jesus' time, suggesting that some diseases are a "judgment from God" (John 9:2).

DEMONIACS: In Mark 5:1–13, a man is said to have "an unclean spirit." He lives among the tombs, and the local people have tried to restrain him there with chains, which he wrenches apart. His self-hatred expresses itself in psychotic public displays of self-wounding rage.

The description of the demoniac recalls many of those who wander the urban sidewalks of North American cities today—people we cross the street to avoid. He has actually marginalized himself. After Jesus cures him, the "crowd" (read "community") arrives and is "afraid" to see the demoniac in his right mind and clothed with dignity. In his book *Poetics of Violence in Mark* Robert Hamerton-Kelly suggests that the demoniac's cure threatens the complacency of his community's existence.[2] No longer out of sight in the tombs (where they may have restrained him as much to keep him from away from public view as to keep him from hurting himself), his presence among them bears witness to their lack of caring and their callous acceptance and even complicity in his state.

Those who suffer from drug, alcohol, and sexual additions also carry a social stigma in our society. There are still people within our society who attribute the addictions of others to a character flaw rather than to a disease. Individuals who suffer from mental illnesses, including depression and schizophrenia, may be judged to have a weakness rather than a disease that needs treatment and understanding. When the behavior of others does not fit within our concept of respectable public behavior, we seek ways to have them hidden from view in different neighborhoods or in institutions.

Those excluded because of social status: the poor and vulnerable.

THE WIDOW OF NAIN: In Luke 7:11–17, Jesus meets a funeral procession at the gate of a town called Nain. A widow's only son has just died. Not only has she lost her last family member, but also with her son dead and no hope of remarrying in Jewish culture, she is doomed to hopeless poverty.

As in most of human history, widows and orphaned children were probably the most vulnerable people in Jesus' world. In a society that distributed wealth, identity, and power through adult males, to be a widow or orphan left an individual destitute, nameless, and powerless. Jewish law recognized this, and included prohibitions against taking advantage of widows and orphans (Exodus 22:21–24; Deuteronomy 10:17–30; Jeremiah 7:6–7). Jesus repeatedly used encounters with and stories about widows to remind his listeners of God's preference on behalf of those most vulnerable (Mark 12:42–43; Luke 1:52–53). His compassion and his action in raising the widow's son to life is a clear sign to the community that their call is also to be aware and responsive to the needs of the helpless in their midst.

Today in the United States, while the standard of living has risen for some Americans, the gap between the rich and the poor has become even greater. One in five children in the United States grows up in poverty. As in Jesus' time, single mothers and their dependent children make up a large percentage of the poorest of our society. Efforts to push people off welfare without regard to their ability to support themselves create a devastating situation for the children of single parents. For Christians, the issue is not about how or why single mothers with dependent children are present in our society. The Gospel issue is how we who are Christians can best support and empower them, bringing God's mercy and compassion and justice to their lives. For a Christian, any policy around welfare must begin with the needs of the young, the weak, and the powerless, not with those who are already in a strong position.

Those excluded for marginalizing behavior: unredeemable sinners.

THE WOMAN WHO ANOINTS JESUS' HAIR: Luke 7:37–50 tells of a banquet that Jesus attends at the home of a religious leader. A woman described as "a sinner" enters, anoints his feet with oil, and dries them with her hair. The story does not tell us what "sin" the woman has committed, but it is clear from the story that, because of her reputation, Jesus' host would not have chosen to have her present at the banquet. Jesus points out that the woman's actions reveal a compassionate spirit that is lacking in the host. When Jesus says, "her sins, which were many, have been forgiven; hence she has shown great love," he reveals how those at the margins of respectability can speak to us who often consider ourselves respectable and virtuous. Those who live at the most extreme edges of sin and forgiveness help all of us to understand how God's mercy can transform lives and how those lives can transform the rest of us.

THE WOMAN CAUGHT IN ADULTERY: In John 8:1–11, the Jewish religious leaders bring a woman discovered in adultery before Jesus. Their sole purpose is to trap Jesus; they show no concern for the woman beyond her use in their plot. According to Jewish law, a woman caught in adultery is to be stoned (Ezekiel 16:38–40). Jesus does not even answer the religious leaders directly. While he respects the law and commands his followers to obey it faithfully, he never allows the law to be used to demean or batter an individual. While Jesus commands her to repent ("from now on do not sin again") he makes it clear that he does not condemn her. He uses the woman's condition to humble and chastise the religious leaders for their own inflated self-images and pretended virtues. He knows that the woman's life—a sinner on the margins of Jewish society—provides a sign and witness to the heart of those consider themselves to be righteous about their need for God's mercy and forgiveness.

THE TAX COLLECTOR: When Jesus passed through Jericho, Luke 19:1–10 tells us, he encountered Zacchaeus, a chief tax collector. Tax collectors were among the most reviled people in Israel. As Jews who worked for the oppressive Roman authority, they were seen by Jewish society as both traitors and parasites. Jesus was not oblivious to the reputation of tax collectors in his society (Matthew 5:46; 18:17) or unaware of his reputation for associating with them (Luke 7:34). Yet he counted them among his closest disciples (Matthew 9:9–11).

Knowing that Zacchaeus would not expect him to accept an invitation, Jesus invites himself to Zacchaeus' house. Jesus' compassionate gesture, risking the criticism of others (Luke 7:7) in order to dine with Zacchaeus, is sufficient to bring about a conversion in the tax collector. He offers to give half of his possessions to the poor and repay four times over anyone he has defrauded. Zacchaeus' extraordinary vow of conversion is the "great love shown by those who have been forgiven much" (Luke 7:47). Those like Zacchaeus who were written off by Jesus' society were the very people whom Jesus sought, forgave, and empowered.

Over the past decades in the United States, many states have passed increasingly harsh sentencing guidelines for those convicted of crimes. Many people, including many of those who would call themselves good Christians, consider the death penalty an acceptable punishment. Can the followers of Jesus, who seek to live as he lived—forgiving even those who put him to death—ever condone such a punishment?

The proportion of people of color in U.S. prisons is much higher than their representation in the larger society. We must all ask ourselves if our justice is God's justice. Just as the Gerasenes found it convenient to lock the demoniac away from sight among the tombs (Mark 5:3–4), we have found it easier in many cases to lock away those whose presence makes us aware of the injustice within our own society.

Those excluded because of ethnicity.

Jewish law forbade discrimination or oppression against non-Jews. The Torah reminded the Jews that they "were aliens in the land of Egypt" (Exodus 22:21; Deuteronomy 10:18). At the same time, the Pentateuch forbade any contact between Jews and foreign women (Deuteronomy 7:1–4; Numbers 25:1–8), and, like any society in any time, those outside of the tribe were often excluded, oppressed, and hated because of their ethnicity.

THE SYROPHOENICIAN WOMAN'S DAUGHTER: In Mark 7:24–30, Jesus is in Tyre, outside of Israel. A woman approaches him, begging him to heal her daughter. At the beginning of this story, it appears that Jesus will not respond to the plea from this foreign woman. Jewish religious law would support him in this stance—a Jewish man would normally not be allowed or expected to associate with a foreign woman. Yet her persistence wins him over. Jesus is challenged by this invitation from a person at the margins of his religious and community world, and his response widens the vision of the reign of God for both of them.

THE SAMARITAN LEPER: In Jesus' time there was strong enmity and little contact between the Jews and the Samaritans (see Matthew 10:5; Luke 9:52–54). In the Gospel of John, Jesus' enemies call him a "Samaritan possessed by a demon" to discredit him (John 8:48). It is precisely the intense Jewish dislike for the Samaritans that makes Jesus' parable about the Good Samaritan (Luke 10:30–37) so powerful to Jewish listeners, contrasting the compassionate actions of this unacceptable and ostracized person with the lack of care shown by the religious leaders of his society. Jesus treats Samaritans with the same care and concern that he gives to those of his own tribe.

In Luke 17:11–19, Jesus heals ten lepers, sending them off to show themselves to the priests, as required by law. When they discover on the way that they are healed, only one of them, a Samaritan, turns back to praise God and give thanks to Jesus. The Samaritan leper in this story is doubly outcast; he is not only separated by his physical affliction, but also by his ethnicity. Yet we are told that he is the only one to return to Jesus and give thanks. The other nine lepers, all presumably Jewish, would be accepted back into Jewish society once they had presented themselves. Jesus says to the Samaritan leper, "Your faith has made you well," even though all ten lepers had been cured. For Jesus, wholeness includes recognizing God's grace and mercy, and responding in gratitude. The story suggests that only someone at the very edges of acceptability can fully understand their complete dependence upon God and express true thankfulness.

THE SAMARTIAN WOMAN: Resting at a well in Samaria on his journey, Jesus meets a woman who has come to draw water. In this encounter (John 4:7–26), Jesus should have avoided contact with the woman because she was Samaritan, and a Jewish man should not have a conversation with a woman in public. The woman is converted not only by Jesus' prophetic telling of her story, but by the fact that he, who should have refused to speak with her, is truly interested in her and in her healing and wholeness. When she becomes convinced that he is the Messiah, she returns to town and is able to convert "many Samaritans because of [her] testimony" (John 4:39).

Jesus understood that people who are broken and outcast have a unique openness to God's grace and mercy. Those who have known rejection and cruelty and discrimination are often more appreciative and receptive to forgiveness, healing, and pardon than those who believe themselves well. That is why he could say to the religious leaders of his time that "tax collectors and the prostitutes are going into the kingdom of God ahead of you" (Matthew 21:31). He knew that his ministry of healing and reconciliation— the same ministry to which we are all called—was primarily for those who had the most to gain from it (Matthew 9:12).

Even within our "enlightened and democratic society" today, there are many who suffer a similar social stigma, isolation, and discrimination to that of the Samaritans in Jesus' time. Gay and lesbian members of our community often find that the Christian virtues of welcome and acceptance do not extend to them. Women in the Roman Catholic Church learn that equality does not include the opportunity to pastor in the same way as a man, while in some communities the divorced and remarried are often excluded from the table of Jesus.

From our safe distance of 2,000 years and many intervening cultures, we may find it easy to pass a harsh judgment on the Jewish establishment of Jesus' time. Why didn't they share his compassionate caring for the marginalized people in these stories? However, when we recast these stories in modern terms, we quickly perceive how little has changed among those of us who are at the "heart" of religious communities and ministries.

Jesus said, "I came into this world for judgment so that those who do not see may see, and those who do see may become blind." Some of the Pharisees near him heard this and said to him, "Surely we are not blind, are we?" Jesus said to them, "If you were blind, you would not have sin. But now that you say, 'We see,' your sin remains."

– John 9:39–41

All of us are in need of God's grace and pardon. But often those of us at the "center" of parish life are unable to see our own needs. Many times it is those who are at the margins of our community and society who best teach us about our common need for repentance, forgiveness, and reconciliation. It is at the margins—the desert places, the desert experiences, in sinners and poets and prophets—that we most powerfully encounter the living God.

Many churches in North America today have defined their mission as "reaching out to the unchurched." In their enthusiasm, they often refashion their worship to reflect an experience that resembles the comfortable and familiar ambience of the concert hall, theater, and TV room. But the phrase "growing at the margins" should not be understood as a mandate simply to attract numbers into our congregations. Rather, "growing" should be understood as the community's growth in depth of understanding, wisdom, vision, and sensitivity to those who are most helpless and rejected—precisely those in whom Jesus tells us he abides (Matthew 25:34–40). Rather than simply offering comfortable entertainment, the Gospel calls the leaders of Christian prayer to fashion worship that echoes Jesus' challenge—to serve "the least of my brothers and sisters."

Several years ago, a parish council member told the pastor, "We don't need wheelchair access because no one in our parish is in a wheelchair." Of course, no one in a wheelchair will ever join that church! For those of us who reside at the "center," our ministry is fulfilled only when we identify with those who are the most vulnerable, including those outside of our community. The vulnerable and weak, with their unique gifts and insights, will never become part of our community until we offer a clear and whole-hearted welcome.

To serve as Jesus did is always to keep our focus outward—to the edges of our congregations, the marginalized of our communities, and the weakest and most vulnerable of our society. It is there that we truly serve in the name and the spirit of Jesus. Indeed, it is there that we serve Jesus himself (Matthew 25:40).

HEAD WORK: DEFINING THE MARGINS

Learn where the margins are.

The call of the Gospel is to seek out those who are most vulnerable and in need (Luke 4:18–19). For Christians today, that means a concerted effort to identify and serve those people—in our parish community, in our neighborhoods, and in the larger society around us. Unfortunately, much of American society is still structured to segregate people of different socioeconomic status and ethnic background. Our call as ministers is to seek out those in our midst who are for us the image of Christ (Matthew 25:31–40). This means not only paying close attention to the news, but also making the extra effort to educate ourselves as to where and how the poorest and most distressed members of our community live.

HEART WORK: DEVELOPING COMPASSION

Put faces on the marginalized.

It is hard to feel compassion for someone who is nameless to us, someone we pass silently on the street or see from a distance. When we come to know someone as a unique, wonderful, and gifted human being, we can no longer ignore his or her suffering.

For example, Larry was a music minister in an affluent suburban parish in the Twin Cities. He was talented and dedicated, and the community appreciated his gifts. At the end of mass one Sunday, he stood before the community with his pastor and said to the congregation, "I need to tell you that I am gay. I have AIDS, and I am dying." Because Larry knew that this would be a very difficult task, he had asked a number of friends to be present at the liturgy. As the congregation was filing out, a friend of Larry's heard one parishioner say to another, "I'm not sure how I feel about gay people, but I know that I love Larry."[3]

Once we know someone, we learn that his or her suffering and need are also our own burdens.

HANDIWORK: ENGAGING THE MARGINS AND THE MARGINALIZED

Serving and celebrating the margins.

Create opportunities for the members of your liturgical ministry—whether musicians, lectors, eucharistic ministers, or liturgy committee members—to volunteer regularly at a local service agency. People who have entered into volunteer service with the intention of "helping others" typically find that their own lives are enriched by their encounters with others. For those of us who lead others in worship, it is a critically important factor in helping us remember what our calling is.

---

1. Walter Brueggemann, *The Prophetic Imagination* (Philadelphia: Fortress Press, 1978), 25.
2. Robert G. Hamerton-Kelly, *Poetics of Violence in Mark* (Minneapolis: Fortress Press, 1994), 93.
3. From a conversation with Madeliene Sue Martin.

SENDING: BLESSED TO BE A BLESSING

Feeding the Whole Body

8

"The king will say to those at his right hand, 'Come, you that are blessed . . . for I was hungry and you gave me food, I was thirsty and you gave me something to drink, I was a stranger and you welcomed me, I was naked and you gave me clothing, I was sick and you took care of me, I was in prison and you visited me.' Then the righteous will answer him, 'Lord, when was it that we saw you hungry and gave you food, or thirsty and gave you something to drink? And when was it that we saw you a stranger and welcomed you, or naked and gave you clothing? And when was it that we saw you sick or in prison and visited you?' And the king will answer them, 'Truly I tell you, just as you did it to one of the least of these who are members of my family, you did it to me.'"

— Matthew 25:34–40

At the end of our Sunday worship, the community is sent forth to love and serve in the name and the spirit of Jesus. Normally this is a very simple and short event; if we have truly gathered as Christ's body, broken open the Word with passion and faithfulness, and celebrated the sacred meal with reverence, richness, faithfulness, and true understanding, our mission will be not only clear but compelling.

In the past six chapters, we have examined six characteristics of Jesus' ministry:

- Attempting to be present to every person and situation.
- Allowing the Spirit to turn us continually toward a deeper life of faith.
- Connecting ourselves to the great stories of our faith and their meaning for us.

- Opening ourselves to a life of deep invitation and response.
- Drawing perspective from the wisdom of those who have shaped our living prayer.
- Identifying with the most vulnerable of our community and society.

If we undertake each of these dimensions of ministry seriously, we will inevitably be challenged and drawn into a life of service that addresses the real needs of others. Following Jesus faithfully means serving as he served. Jesus' life was a continuous expression of healing, feeding, empowering, comforting, and liberating. He did not stay in the synagogue, but went out to the edges of Jewish society and beyond, doing works of mercy and justice. Indeed, Jesus defined the heart of his ministry as a connection of the proclamation of the Good News of God's reign with acts of mercy, healing, and restoration.

> When John heard in prison what the Messiah was doing, he sent word by his disciples and said to him, "Are you the one who is to come, or are we to wait for another?" Jesus answered them, "Go and tell John what you hear and see: the blind receive their sight, the lame walk, the lepers are cleansed, the deaf hear, the dead are raised, and the poor have good news brought to them" (Matthew 11:2–5).

It is also significant that, even within the synagogue, Jesus ministered to the whole person, and he seems to indicate that ritual observance (i.e., liturgy) is subject to ministering to the real needs and well-being of others.

> He left that place and entered their synagogue; a man was there with a withered hand, and they asked him, "Is it lawful to cure on the Sabbath?" so that they might accuse him. He said to them, "Suppose one of you has only one sheep and it falls into a pit on the Sabbath; will you not lay hold of it and lift it out? How much more valuable is a human being than a sheep! So it is lawful to do good on the Sabbath." Then he said to the man, "Stretch out your hand." He stretched it out, and it was restored, as sound as the other (Matthew 12:9–13).

In Jesus, leadership roles in community prayer and attention to the very real needs of individuals cannot be separated. Authentic worship demands authentic caring for those within and outside of our gatherings. The life of anyone who follows Jesus is a continuing call to serve and care for others as he did, ministering to bodies as well as spirits. In serving the real needs of others, it is important that we treat all with the dignity with which we would treat Christ. If we truly perceive Christ as present in others, we will never act from the condescending position that we are doing some good for others. Rather, we will act out of gratitude and love in response to the love that has been shown to us and the awareness that God is most powerfully and fully present to us in those we serve. In serving others, we may discover that those we serve minister to us, opening our hearts and minds to an awareness of God's sacred reign.

"There is still one thing lacking. Sell all that you own and distribute the money to the poor, and you will have treasure in heaven; then come, follow me."

– Luke 18:22

"When you give a banquet, invite the poor, the crippled, the lame, and the blind. And you will be blessed, because they cannot repay you."

– Luke 14:13

THE REIGN OF GOD WILL BE LIKE THIS!

In the last chapter, we had a brief glimpse of the story in which Jesus heals a man of leprosy, a disease that had separated him from his own community (Mark 1:40–45). Jesus did not think of the man as unclean—indeed, he touches the man *before* he has been healed of his leprosy. But Jesus heals the man's body and names him clean because he knows that the Jewish society of his time would not consider the man as clean (nor would the leper consider himself clean) until his body was healed. Jesus gave dignity back to the man through healing his whole body. His anger was directed at those who would exclude a person because of his physical infirmities.

Worship is the place in which Christians proclaim, "The reign of God will be like this!" For this reason, our liturgies are often filled with words of hope and comfort for those who suffer from lack of housing, lack of opportunity, hunger, and discrimination. If we believe that our responsibility as ministers ends with the naming of these issues, our worship is not true and faithful to the Gospel of Jesus. If our proclamation of justice and mercy for all is not consistent with our actions, we distort and limit both our own vision and the vision of our communities about what the reign of God is to be.

> What good is it, my brothers and sisters, if you say you have faith but do not have works? Can faith save you? If a brother or sister is naked and lacks daily food, and one of you says to them, "Go in peace; keep warm and eat your fill," and yet you do not supply their bodily needs, what is the good of that? (James 2:14–16)

If leaders of prayer allow our worship to be only lip service to the needs of others, our prayer becomes inward and self-serving. It is no wonder that the prophet Amos railed so strongly against what he perceived as worship without justice.

> I hate, I despise your festivals, and I take no delight in your solemn assemblies. Even though you offer me your burnt offerings and grain offerings, I will not accept them; and the offerings of well-being of your fatted animals I will not look upon. Take away from me the noise of your songs; I will not listen to the melody of your harps. But let justice roll down like waters, and righteousness like an ever-flowing stream (Amos 5:21–24).

Authentic worship only happens in communities in which genuine needs are named and served. If we hold up the needs of others in our prayers, but do not work to heal and nourish and defend others, our very words within worship will indict us. And this service is not only or even primarily for those within our community; rather, our task is to continually widen the circle of our concern to include the vulnerable and needy wherever they are.

Once a pastor had introduced a period of prayer at each Sunday gathering for particular individuals in the parish and the surrounding community who were suffering, and a parishioner complained that it added too much time to the liturgy. The pastor reminded him that focusing on the needs of others is the very heart of our prayer, *not an option to choose or omit as we wish.*[1]

HEAD WORK: DEVELOPING INTO WHOLE PEOPLE

Seeking wholeness in our own lives.

A number of years ago, my wife, Linda, and I jointly presented a workshop on balancing professional and personal life. Linda spoke first: "Marty should not be giving this workshop," she said. "He should be taking it." Effective ministry is made much easier when we are strong, clear, and balanced in our spiritual and personal lives. A regular rhythm of prayer, healthy life practices, a circle of friends, and a community of believers to hold us up when our own belief falters are critical to our ability to minister to others.

HEART WORK: FINDING AND NAMING THE NEEDS

Inform yourself about community and global needs.

The Christian who seeks to follow Jesus must make the effort to discern the needs of the neighborhood, the city, and the world. It is our Christian responsibility to stay informed about the critical needs of others and seek creative ways to assist them.

HANDIWORK: EMPOWERING AND CHALLENGING OUR COMMUNITIES

Build a fire in your assembly.

Jesus called his followers to be servants, but not helpless or docile. Indeed, he empowered his followers, making them strong healers, teachers, and prophets. The best ministers work wholeheartedly to empower the members of their communities. The Gospel of Jesus challenges us to be active in our service to others, and to challenge each other to greater service. Do not be afraid to let the words and songs of our worship call us to a greater commitment. Most often, the lack of passion within our worship and our communities comes not because we ask too much, but because we do not ask enough.

1. Offered by Bonnie Faber.

Selected Bibliography for Those Who Plan and Lead Worship

Foundational Reading

For Roman Catholics

The Liturgy Documents. Vol. 1. 4th ed. Chicago: Liturgy Training
    Publications, 2004.
——. Vol. 2. Chicago: Liturgy Training Publications, 2000.
The Liturgy Documents provides the central documents on liturgy
produced by the Roman Catholic Church since the Second Vatican Council.

*The Music Documents: Music in Catholic Worship & Liturgical Music
    Today.* Washington, DC: United States Conference of Catholic
    Bishops, 1982.
These documents provide a short and clear introduction to liturgy for
anyone involved in worship leadership. These two documents are also
included in *The Liturgy Documents*, Vol. 1. These documents can be
purchased together in one book from Oregon Catholic Press (Portland,
Oregon).

The Milwaukee Symposia for Church Composers: A Ten-Year Project.
    Washington, DC: National Association of Pastoral Musicians and
    Chicago: Liturgy Training Publications, 1992.
Available from Oregon Catholic Press (Portland, Oregon).

Duchesneau, Claude, and Michel Veuthey. *Music and Liturgy: The
    Universa Laus Document and Commentary.* Washington, DC:
    The Pastoral Press, 1992.
Available from Oregon Catholic Press (Portland, Oregon).

For Lutherans and Mainline Protestants

The following publications are part of the Renewing Worship process in the
ELCA (Evangelical Lutheran Church in America); they provide excellent
foundational reading for anyone involved in liturgical ministry. They are all
published through Augsburg Fortress Press (Minneapolis):

The Use of the Means of Grace (1997)
Congregational Song (2001)

Principles for Worship (2002)
Holy Baptism and Related Rites (2002)
Holy Communion and Related Rites (2004)
The Church's Year (2004)
Daily Prayer (2004)

History and Development of Christian Liturgy and Music

Cabié, Robert. *History of the Mass*. Washington, DC: The Pastoral
　　Press, 1992.
Available from Oregon Catholic Press.

Foley, Edward. *From Age to Age*. Chicago: Liturgy Training
　　Publications, 1991.

Macy, Gary. *The Banquet's Wisdom*. New York: Paulist Press, 1992.

White, James F. *Introduction to Christian Worship*. Rev. ed. Nashville:
　　Abingdon Press, 1990.

Wilson-Dickson, Andrew. *The Story of Christian Music*. Minneapolis:
　　Augsburg Fortress, 2003.

Scripture and Ministry

Brueggemann, Walter. *Israel's Praise: Doxology against Idolatry*.
　　Philadelphia: Fortress Press, 1978.

———. *The Message of the Psalms*. Minneapolis: Augsburg Fortress
　　Press, 1984.

Erlander, Daniel. *Manna and Mercy/A Brief History of God's Unfolding
　　Promise to Mend the Entire Universe*. Whitby Island, WA: The
　　Order of Saints Martin and Teresa, 1992. (360-331-4066)

Wren, Brian. *What Language Shall I Borrow?/God-Talk in Worship: A
　　Male Response to Feminist Theology*. New York: Crossroad,
　　1989.

Leadership in Worship

Bell, John L. *The Singing Thing/A Case for Congregational Singing.* Chicago: GIA   Publications, 2000.

Dawn, Marva. *Reaching Out without Dumbing Down.* Grand Rapids, MI: Eerdmans, 1995.

Farlee, Robert Buckley, ed. *Leading the Church's Song.* Minneapolis: Augsburg Fortress, 1998.

————. *Musicians in the Assembly: A Worship Handbook.* Minneapolis: Augsburg Fortress, 2001.

Haas, David. *Music and the Mass/A Practical Guide for Ministers of Music.* Chicago: Liturgy Training Publications, 1998.

Hook, M. Anne Burnette. *Grace Notes: Spirituality and the Choir.* Nashville: Discipleship Resources, 1998.

Johnson, Lawrence J. *The Ministers of Music.* Washington, DC: National Association of Pastoral Musicians, 1983.
Available from Oregon Catholic Press (Portland,OR).

Widening the Circle: Designing Worship That Reaches. Minneapolis: Augsburg Fortress, 2001.

Westermeyer, Paul. *The Church Musician.* Rev. ed. Minneapolis: Augsburg Fortress, 1997.

Worship Planning

For Roman Catholics

Living Liturgy, published annually by the Liturgical Press (Collegeville, MN).

Sourcebook for Sundays and Seasons, published annually by Liturgy Training Publications (Chicago).

For Lutherans and Mainline Protestants

Sundays and Seasons, published annually (Minneapolis: Augsburg Fortress).

Seasons of the Spirit, published annually (Cleveland: United Church Press).

United Methodist Music and Worship Planner, published annually (Nashville: Abingdon Press).

Imaging the Word: An Arts and Lectionary Resource. Vol. 1–3. (Cleveland: United Church Press).

Reflections on Worship

Brueggemann, Walter. *The Prophetic Imagination*. Philadelphia: Fortress Press, 1978.

Collins, Dori Erwin and Scott C. Weidler. *Sound Decisions: Evaluating Contemporary Music for Lutheran Worship*. Minneapolis: Augsburg Fortress, 1997.

Huck, Gabe. *Liturgy with Style and Grace*. Chicago: Liturgy Training Publications, 1984.

Lathrop, Gordon W. *Holy Ground/A Liturgical Cosmology*. Minneapolis: Augsburg Fortress, 2003.

———. *Holy People/A Liturgical Ecclesiology*. Minneapolis: Augsburg Fortress, 1999.

———. *Holy Things: A Liturgical Theology*. Minneapolis: Augsburg Fortress, 1993.

Nelson-Pallmeyer, Jack, and Bret Hesla. *Worship in the Spirit of Jesus/Theology, Liturgy and Songs without Violence*. Cleveland: Pilgrim Press, 2005.

Schattauer, Thomas, ed. *Inside Out: Worship in an Age of Mission*, Minneapolis: Augsburg Fortress, 1999.

Saliers, Don E. *Worship and Spirituality*. Rev. ed. Akron, OH: OSL Publications, 1996.

———. *Worship Come to Its Senses*. Nashville: Abingdon Press, 1996.

Words for Worship

Duck, Ruth. *Touch Holiness*. Cleveland: United Church Press, 1990.

Iona Community. *Wee Worship Book*. Chicago: GIA Publications, 1999.

Taizé Community. *Prayer for Each Day*. Chicago: GIA Publications, 1998.

Tirabassi, Maren, and Kathy Wonson Eddy. *Gift of Many Cultures/ Worship Resources for the Global Community*. Cleveland: Pilgrim Press, 1995.

Workbook for Lectors and Gospel Readers (Revised Common Lectionary). Chicago: Liturgy Training Publications.

Worship and Culture

Bass, Dorothy C. *Receiving the Day*. San Francisco: Jossey-Bass, 2000.

Gaillarde, Richard R. *Transforming Our Days*. New York: Crossroad, 2000.

Other books by Marty Haugen, available from GIA Publications:

Instrumentation and the Liturgical Ensemble

Turn My Heart/A Sacred Journey from Brokenness to Healing
    (with Susan Briehl)

MARTY HAUGEN is a liturgical composer and workshop presenter. His music appears in Roman Catholic and Protestant hymnals in a number of countries.

Haugen lives in Eagan, Minnesota, with his wife, Linda. They have two children.